The Federal Judiciary and Institutional Change

The Federal Judiciary and Institutional Change

Deborah J. Barrow,
Gary Zuk, and
Gerard S. Gryski

Ann Arbor
THE UNIVERSITY OF MICHIGAN PRESS

Published in the United States of America by
The University of Michigan Press
Manufactured in the United States of America
♾ Printed on acid-free paper

1999 1998 1997 1996 4 3 2 1

A CIP catalog record for this book is available from the British Library.

Library of Congress Cataloging-in-Publication Data

Barrow, Deborah J., 1952–
The federal judiciary and institutional change / Deborah J. Barrow, Gary Zuk, and Gerard S. Gryski.
p. cm.
Includes index.
ISBN 0-472-10634-1 (hardcover : alk. paper)
1. Courts—United States—History. 2. Coalition governments—United States—History. 3. Law and politics—History. I. Zuk, Gary, 1950– . II. Gryski, Gerard S. III. Title.
KF8719.B35 1996
347.73′1′09—dc20
[347.307109] 96-5994
CIP

To Evelyn Hughes (D.J.B.)

To the loving memory of Emilie
Streble Godfrey and Lee Zuk (G.Z.)

To my parents, Anna and Casmir Gryszkiewicz (G.S.G.)

Contents

Tables

Figures

Acknowledgments

This volume could not have been completed were it not for the generous assistance and cooperation of a number of individuals and organizations. The Law and Social Science program of the National Science Foundation funded a major portion of the data collection (NSF grant SBR-9311999). We are ever grateful to program officers Susan White and Neal Tate for their support and encouragement of our work. The Senate Judiciary Committee staffs of Senators Joseph Biden (D–DE) and Howell Heflin (D–AL) graciously provided us with access to the public questionnaires of judicial nominees from the Carter through Bush presidencies. This information was supplemented by government documents in the archives of Draughon Library at Auburn University, many of which were acquired specifically for our study. We are indebted to Dianne Bradley, Boyd Childress, Anna Coffman, Tim Dodge, Janet Frederick, Jim Gravois, Yvonne Kozlowski, Joyce Ledbetter, Harmon Straiton, Lin Thornton, Lorna Wiggins, and Lanelle Wills, for both procuring information needed to conduct research and providing a working place to store and review these materials. The Office of Vice President for Research and Dean of the College of Liberal Arts defrayed part of the expense of the project and advised us throughout. We especially appreciate the good counsel and assistance of Paul Parks, Gordon Bond, John Heilman, and Gerald Johnson. Thanks as well to our colleagues in the Department of Political Science for their forbearance during the writing of this book, and particularly to our department head, Cal Clark, who gave us professional and personal guidance throughout. We owe a substantial debt to Bruce Reed of the Division of University Computing for his technical assistance, to Blair Hobbs for indexing, and to Malcolm Litchfield and the staff of the University of Michigan Press who brought this book to fruition. Professor Sheldon Goldman of the University of Massachusetts has been a continuing source of help and support of our research. Virginia Prickett performed her usual word processing wizardry on the manuscript. Of course none of the organizations or individuals mentioned above bears any responsibility for any of the interpretations, conclusions, or errors found in this volume.

The authors variously want to take this opportunity to thank family and friends for their devotion and encouragement. Barrow: As always I am grateful for the support of my family—Emma, Gene, Blake, Kathy, Jake, and Brett Barrow. I also thank Jim Ballard for his constant encouragement. I am also indebted to certain administrative staff and faculty of Emory University School of Law, Anne Rector, Celeste Katz, Professor Deb Cohen, and Associate Dean Nathaniel Gozansky, who were invaluable sources of inspiration during this time. Special appreciation goes to my friends and law school classmates, and in particular to the following professors whose guidance has been essential to opening a new intellectual process to my thinking—Dean Howard O. Hunter, John Witte, Frank J. Vandall, and for his special ability to educate, William T. Mayton. Zuk: I would like to acknowledge my everlasting appreciation and affection for family and friends whose good cheer and best wishes were a happy part of this endeavor: my wife, Rose, parents, Marian and Frank, brother, Kurt, and dear companions Harold Clarke, Mike Conniff, Janet Frederick, Jim Godfrey, Jim Hollifield, Marianne Stewart, and Dan and Jan Szechi. Gryski: My sister and brother, Eileen Byrnes and Marty Gryski, continue to be a source of inspiration. I would also like to thank Laura Bell, Donna Bohanan, Joe Clark, Rick Cook, Allen DeCotiis, Charles Markle, Frank Smith, Larry Stafford, and especially the political science faculty of the University of Massachusetts for giving me a chance.

CHAPTER 1

Partisan and Institutional Change on the Federal Courts

> History matters. It matters not just because we can learn from the past, but because the present and the future are connected to the past by the continuity of a society's institutions. Today's and tomorrow's choices are shaped by the past. And the past can only be made intelligible as a story of institutional evolution.
>
> —Douglass C. North

When Ulysses Grant entered the White House in 1869 there were 61[1] federal judges. The major issues before the courts involved the constitutionality of the Republican Reconstruction program.[2] By the time George Bush left office, the legal community was hotly debating the question of whether the federal bench should be capped at 1,000 judges. Judges were grappling with divisive social issues such as affirmative action and scientific matters engendered by a veritable explosion in technology, and in the offing were ominous questions about the legality of scientific breakthroughs such as genetic engineering. Potential appointees were sometimes "screened" for their positions on issues important to presidents, and in other instances the goal of diversifying the bench by race and gender was placed at the forefront.

We obviously have witnessed a radical transformation in the size and subject matter of the federal judiciary from Reconstruction to the age of "the information superhighway." In this volume we explain the mechanics of this transformation and how they have been driven by political factors. Our concern here is with deciphering the institutional arrangements for and the politics of staffing the bench. Although the accoutrements of the process have certainly evolved, the rudiments date from the founding of the Republic. Kelly and Harbison offer this observation on Grant's first two appointees to the High Court:

> Grant's action differed little or not at all from that of all Presidents making appointments to the Court, since Presidents invariably consider the constitutional, political, and economic implications of their judicial appointments.[3]

Then, as now, presidents endeavored to place an imprint on the courts that would long survive their own tenure in office. Then, as now, confirmation was subject to the "Advice and Consent" of the Senate. In the chapters that follow, we discern cycles—indeed rhythm—in the partisan transformation of the third branch that are conditioned by whether or not the other two are in the hands of the same party. The stage on which the drama is played out, however, rests upon the institutional protocols for staffing the bench, which are sometimes radically rearranged.

We offer explanations for the institutional changes transpiring over the modern history of the third branch. Ours is a broad-brush approach, in which we step back to obtain the widest possible angle to observe the ongoing dynamics of internal adjustments in the judiciary's membership and the contextual influences on its structure. Here we broach the major questions guiding the analyses presented in chapters 2 through 5, along with the conceptual framework of institutionalism, the tradition into which our work falls. Following this the core concepts of the subject of inquiry are developed.

This study is the first systematic treatment of the organizational development of the modern federal court system. Beginning with the inception of a stable two-party system in 1869 through the close of the 102d Congress in 1992, we examine the influence of the president, Congress, and the judges themselves in shaping the institutional features and membership of the lower federal bench. Institutional transformation is assessed under varying political conditions (that is, unified versus divided party governance), over time, and during three historical epochs: 1869–1932, 1933–68, and 1969–92. These three periods are distinguished by the degree to which one party dominated the American political scene and so influenced the contours of the federal judiciary. Despite a recent spate of scholarly works on divided government,[4] its impact on the partisan and institutional features of the third branch has received no attention. Our compilation of data on over 2,500 federal judges, spanning 62 congresses and 24 presidential administrations, enables us to address this issue.

Our interest in the evolution of the federal courts grew out of curiosity peaked by the dramatic partisan transformation of the judiciary from 1981 to 1992. Indeed, at the adjournment of the 102d Congress, over 70 percent of all federal judges were members of the Republican Party. Moreover, 95 percent of this cohort were the appointees of only two presidents, Ronald Reagan and George Bush.

Obvious questions arise. Are these lopsided figures unusual or even extraordinary? How does the partisan reconfiguring of the federal courts over the last decade compare to previous Republican and Democratic administrations? Might these percentages have been higher still had Reagan and Bush enjoyed unified control during their terms in office, or did they run their party's tally on the bench as far as any president could? This leads to perhaps the most intriguing query of a more general theoretical nature: Given that presidents overwhelmingly appoint judges from their own party, what political conditions and interinstitutional arrangements enlarge opportunities for patronage appointments and thus enhance same-party control of the third branch? Additionally, do the alternative avenues for increasing appointment opportunities vary over time or by party?

These questions take on added importance in light of growing complaints from the judiciary that the leaving rate of its members is reaching crisis proportions.[5] Moreover, an inordinate percentage of those taking senior status through retirement or relinquishing their position completely through resignation were doing so at a younger age and with fewer years of service, suggesting a possible change in the political and professional perspectives on life tenure.

Another source of organizational stress and strain is the rapid rate of growth in the size of the bench. Since Reconstruction, the number of judges has doubled approximately every 30 years.[6] In some respects bench expansion mirrors that of government generally, but it is also distinctive in its rate, causes, and consequences. Indeed, the third branch is now one and one-half times the size of Congress; factoring in senior status (retired judges who continue to work, but with reduced caseloads), it is twice the size.

We see, then, an organ of government beset by alternating party control, accelerating turnover, and, perhaps equally important, a constant acculturation of new members through record-breaking growth—dramatic changes for an institution whose constitutional design heralded political independence and stability![7] How, then, have institutional protocols among the three branches changed to produce the discrepancy between the initial and current products? To what extent were the transformations brought on by short-term political expediency or long-run dynamics? Regardless of the source, what consequences (positive or negative) lie in wait if these patterns continue?

Institutions and the Study of Politics

The characteristics, roles, and functions of institutions are the core of American politics that extend beyond constitutions, laws, and other formal arrangements to include informal norms and expectations surrounding them:

> Institutions are the rules of the game in a society or, more formally, are the humanly devised constraints that shape human interaction. In consequence they structure incentives in human exchange, whether political, social, or economic. Institutional change shapes the way societies evolve through time and hence is the key to understanding historical change.[8]

Institutions shape politics as much as the political climate affects them. Although influenced by the actions and interactions of their members, they also take on a life of their own. Formal rules and informal norms structure the ways members behave toward one another, providing cues for individual and collective behavior toward other institutions. Thus, an accurate gauging of the pulse of the American political process comes from an understanding of how political organizations operate and evolve.

Institutions play a predominant role in determining the performance of political, economic, and social systems.[9] They control individual behavior through incentive structures, internal rules, socialization norms, and momentum, thereby serving as the primary causes of continuity or change across generations. Indeed, March and Olsen attribute the actual ordering of political life to these "fundamental features of politics."[10] By structuring the interaction of participants through these various means, institutions lend a degree of predictability to social, economic, and political outcomes, as well as provide the basic rules and processes for change.[11]

The tenets of institutionalism are especially germane to our study. First, the federal judiciary can properly be conceptualized as an organized collectivity interacting with others and affected by political/legal conditions (e.g., caseload increases) in a complex environment. By constitutional and statutory design, each branch of government has authority over the structure and development of the third branch. The president's appointment power is, of course, one of the more direct and influential means of shaping the partisan parameters of the judiciary. The Senate acts both in the formal capacity of its advice and consent authority, and often informally through the custom of courtesy. Congress controls the size of the institution by determining whether additional positions should be created. The first branch also exercises authority over the organization of the federal bench, including the power to create, restructure, or abolish courts, as well as their jurisdictions. Although the Constitution forbids reductions in judicial salaries, Congress can enhance the emoluments of office, such as retirement benefits, salary, and other corporate concerns.[12] The judiciary itself has considerable latitude in matters pertaining to the administration of the courts through the Judicial Conference of the United States and the Administrative Office of the United States Courts. The Conference's ability to influence the legislative agenda, for example, derives in large part from its role in proposing and drafting court-related legislation. The judiciary controls its internal administrative and disciplinary procedures, collects statistical information on federal courts and offices, and assesses its own organizational needs (including judgeships) based on those data. These political and administrative assets give the third branch substantial opportunity and autonomy to affect its structure.

Second, as most of the theoretical and empirical refinements in research focus on individual-level behavior of judges in their adjudicative capacity, attention to the judiciary as an institution has received short shrift.[13] Institutions are more than mere aggregations of individual decisions, though such behavior is one of their important components. Neither are they simply reactive, responding solely to changes in the environment. Instead, organizations actively participate in shaping their world, requiring that they be analyzed in the context of their relationship to other institutions. Our interest in fundamental, broad-based changes in the character of the judiciary, we believe, complements contemporary scholarship on judicial decision making and uses many of its constructs. Most works in the area document party affiliation of the judge and appointing president, for example, as key determinants of the decisional tendencies of federal judges.[14] These same factors might also help illuminate the institutional evolution of the judiciary. There is no reason to expect nor evidence to demonstrate that variables so resilient at one analytical level would be any less so at another.

Institutional Continuity and Change

Understanding the dynamics of institutional change is vital to our undertaking, because they unlock answers to the questions of how and why processes and networks operate as they do.[15] The evolution of the federal judiciary, by and large, is attributable to two types of change agents—structural and political. The importance of the former derives from the authority of each of the three branches of government to alter the size, framework, and membership of the judiciary by both formal and informal means. History is replete with examples of the first and second branches jockeying to change the structure of the third. Yet on occasion such efforts were the sole work of the judiciary itself or of one of its representatives.[16]

A case in point is the Act of February 25, 1919, enabling judges with stipulated years of service to take senior status—that is, to retire with full pay but still hear cases, albeit at reduced levels. Once the specified term of service is reached, the decision to retire is cost-free—a judge sacrifices no pay or benefits and is still able to practice his or her profession. The legislation is a benchmark for the study of partisan transformation of the third branch. As we show, judges often time their departures politically: understanding that their leaving creates opportunities for presidents to replace them, judges are inclined to exit when a president of their party sits in the White House. Thus, the presidents' ability to recast the bench in their own political image was enhanced by an act of Congress that created a method for the institution to be transformed by the behavior of its own "nonpolitical" members.

Institutional change is also a by-product of the political terrain. Of particular significance is the centrifugal effect of divided government, which can stymie otherwise well-conceived strategies for changing the direction of organizational policy. Behaviors might be different under such gridlocked conditions, so one might observe times when the institution is stagnant or changes only marginally. During periods of unified party government, by contrast, the incoming party might initially make abrupt changes that set in motion long-term, permanent alterations in the functioning and status of the targeted institution, with a substantial cumulative impact.

The notion that unified government facilitates action and divided government thwarts it has often taken on the aura of an axiom,[17] when actually the evidence of its impact on institutional and political performance is mixed. Mayhew's comprehensive study of legislative behavior from 1946 to 1990 under conditions of divided and unified government, for example, revealed no significant difference in congressional performance in either the amount or significance of legislation enacted or in congressional oversight of the executive branch. Enactment was attributable less to same-party control of the government and more to timing (first two years of a presidential term) and changes in public mood.[18] Similarly, Davidson found that conditions of party control had little impact on the workload and productivity of the post–World War II Congress.[19]

On the other side of the ledger, Kelly's reanalysis of Mayhew's data (with a reformulated innovative policy measure) showed that divided government made a difference.[20] Rohde and Simon noted, as well, that presidents manifested different veto behavior during such periods,[21] whereas Richardson and Scheb observed that appointments to the Supreme Court under split control led to moderation in civil rights and liberties decisions.[22] Indeed, some scholarly assessments of budgetary politics have concluded that divided government is the root cause of many of the economic ills—particularly large deficits—that have bedeviled the nation throughout the 1980s and into the 1990s.[23]

Instructive as this literature is, it is also problematic, for as Fiorina observes, some studies are much more historically and empirically comprehensive than others, so results often vary because measurements, time periods, and conditions differ.[24] A strength of our study is the ability to evaluate broadly defined institutional measures over the past 125 years. In any case, our goal is different. We do not enter the debate over whether split control is a historical accident, thereby suggesting that government is possibly not working properly or effectively. Nor do we establish the reasons why such conditions exist. Instead we employ government structure as a variable, assessing its effect on the institutional evolution of the third branch.[25]

The Elements of Institutional Change

The judiciary is transformed—gradually or abruptly—either by reconstituting its membership or by restructuring its organizational environment. Membership recomposition occurs when judges are appointed to fill vacancies and positions created by enlarging the bench. Restructuring is generally the result of legislative and administrative changes in staffing procedures. Our composite measure of institutional change is a function of three components—bench expansion, replacements created by voluntary and involuntary departures, and elevations.

Organizational growth is stimulated by internal or environmental changes that are either quantitative (increase in "business") or qualitative (enlargement or upgrading of mission), often connoting alterations in status within the political system as well.[26] Consequently, we learn much about the ranking and the role that an institution has by tracing the evolution of its size. Bench expansion, in the context of the federal judiciary, is a key element in this regard. Judgeships, of course, are life tenure appointments, so with the creation of each one the institution is enlarged.[27] Although we rarely find retractions in the number of judicial offices,[28] we do anticipate that the rate at which judicial positions are legislated and the reasons why will vary over time, especially across historical eras.

Replacement or addition of new members does more than simply change the complexion of an organization. It is a transitional process whereby new ideas, norms, and political and social characteristics modify existing ones.[29] We examine the phenomenon in two ways. First, we explore the distribution of key attributes of the members over time and across subperiods and presidential administrations. This aggregate assessment provides a picture of the institution and a profile of its members. We pay special attention to traits such as party affiliation and appointing president. There are other traits that also are important in gauging how the status of the institution is changing, such as patterns of age at time of appointment and length of tenure. Second, because we are interested in the development of the institution, we analyze how the dynamics among the elements of change move across time. We focus on three types of membership change: appointments to new seats and to vacancies; voluntary (retirements or resignations) and involuntary (deaths in office, impeachments, position abolishments) departures; and elevations.

Appointments. Federal judgeships are important founts of patronage. Accordingly, we consider presidential appointment behavior by examining same-party (as the appointing president) versus cross-party appointments. This comparison plays a crucial part in understanding how the political tides of national politics transform the federal courts. We investigate the degree to which the political landscape, particularly the relationship between Congress and the president, and the latter's public standing, aids an administration's ability to run up its party's tally on the bench. We also give some attention to whether cross-party appointments vary by the source of the position (as new seats or replacements for vacancies).

Replacements. Considerable fanfare attends the enactment of omnibus judgeship legislation. Senators garner opportunities for patronage, and the White House has a chance to stock the bench with jurists who can carry on its policy legacy for years or even decades to come. Vacancies, especially those owing to voluntary departures from the bench, occasion virtually the same results yet draw comparatively little scholarly attention. Yet leaving the bench voluntarily is no less a manifestation of political behavior. Perhaps underlying the lack of appreciation of the politics of turnover is an anachronistic view of a judgeship as being a coveted spot at the apex of the legal profession that one would forsake only for death or serious illness. This image might be sentimental as well, because one increasingly hears complaints from those who wear the ermine about the material and other sacrifices that come with the territory.[30] Indeed, as noted earlier, institutional changes mandate that federal judges can elect to take senior status (and thus give the president the opportunity to appoint a successor), yet still hear cases (at a reduced level) and retain the trappings of office, including pay and benefits. So those eligible to take senior status give up little by timing their departure politically.

The rate at which members are being replaced, and the reason, are excellent cues for determining the extent of internal transformation and the influence that the political arena has on an institution. Investigating the dynamics of turnover along with the background characteristics of those who leave helps us to detect changes in the professional behavior of judges that may also be suggestive of large-scale alteration in their perceptions toward the institution or the office. Scholarly works on the historical development of Congress have found variations in the perceptions of officeholders over time and across subperiods.[31] We draw upon this body of research throughout.

Elevations. Elevations are a subtle means by which presidents can augment the size of their cohort on the courts. The literature nevertheless says little about this species of appointment, even though they are quite interesting from a political standpoint and are becoming more prevalent. Indeed, at the most basic level, if a president makes a nomination to the courts of appeals from outside the judicial system, that of course provides one appointment opportunity and the attendant patronage and political good will. On the other hand, by elevating a sitting district court judge to the next level, a vacancy will open up on the district court and thus this path to filling an appeals court seat will afford two appointments. With judicial selection being interinstitutional in nature, district court judges so nominated approach the Senate with the trump card of having previously been confirmed by that body. Finally, by choosing individuals with established judicial "track records," the White House is in a better position to project the potential nominee's renderings on the appellate bench, or even the U.S. Supreme Court.[32]

This type of appointment behavior, like the others, varies across administrations and under different political conditions. We explore the circumstances under which presidents are more likely to close in the ranks of government appointments and service. Incoming presidents may react differently, for example, when faced with a lopsided partisan balance in the courts and Congress due to a long-run dominance of the opposite party. Or they may be inclined to narrow the appointment base when they have agendas for change that require a high degree of political loyalty or ideological commitment. Equally important, we investigate the extent to which one administration draws on the district court cohort of another, suggesting the possibility of close policy ties between, say, Kennedy and Johnson or Reagan and Bush appointees. Assessing the rate at which presidents elevate their own or their predecessors' appointees against circumstances such as government structure might shed some light on selection strategies.

Institutional Change. Our summary indicator of institutional change benchmarks fluctuations over time and across administrations in the rate of political transformation of the courts under different political and institutional conditions, and is comprised of the three components above. The dynamics behind each of the three are somewhat different because the sources and the effects differ depending on prevailing political conditions. In short, appointments, replacements, and elevations may become alternatives to one another.

This chapter provides the conceptual framework of our work. Chapter 2 is an overview of the third branch's development over the entire period of the study. We spell out and evaluate the hypotheses that are grounds for the analyses in the three chapters that follow. Chapters 3, 4, and 5 each focus on a particular historical era. Chapter 3 investigates the first phase of Republican Party dominance, from 1869 to 1932. During these years the modern methods of staffing the courts developed, as did their structure. Further, the chief institutional actors in this process entered the scene. The chapter also provides the baseline for subsequent examinations of alterations in the institution's characteristics. Chapter 4 explores the transformation of the federal bench during the heyday of the Democratic Party from 1933 to 1968. We contrast changes in this era to the previous one and to the historical means to gauge differences in party governance. This middle era reaffirms the importance of government structure, which this time redounds to the benefit of the Democrats. In chapter 5 we analyze the impact of the most recent period of Republican dominance on the current state of the federal bench. Here we observe the most marked changes in bench size, turnover, scale of appointments, and rate of partisan transformation from 1869 to 1992, all differences of degree that built on and carried over from the previous two eras, yet transpired in an era of often split control of the first and second branches of government. We also see indications of changing career perspectives; for example, contemporary jurists are appointed at a much younger age than their predecessors, but they also have considerably shorter stints on the bench. Finally, in chapter 6 our findings are placed in the context of institutional and neoinstitutional theories of politics. Additionally, we stake out where the evolution of the judiciary since 1869 has brought the institution at the close of the twentieth century.

The impact of presidential elections on court staffing and the causes and effects of the tremendous growth in the size of the institution are important themes for understanding the role of the federal judiciary in modern-day politics. The magnitude of its influence in carrying out presidential initiatives is augmented by the ever-increasing turnover rate, driven predominantly by politically timed retirements. Many of these aspects of the third branch's current status increase its political influence, giving it a more visible and significant role in presidential and partisan politics, while at the same time weakening it in national politics. While perhaps only a small portion of the American electorate is motivated to use its presidential ballot as a referendum on the performance of the federal judiciary, a consequence of the voters' decision to change the party controlling the White House is wholesale political transformation of the federal courts as well.

CHAPTER 2

Past Is Prologue: A Historical Profile of the Federal Bench

> Packing a district court with unneeded judges is not only an economic waste. It is degrading and humiliating to every serving judge in the district affected. . . . Certainly those in authority will wish reason and intelligence as guides, rather than that their action shall be influenced by selfish desires for patronage, moving along ancient log-rolling ways.
>
> —Judge Merrill E. Otis, U.S. District Judge for the Western District of Missouri

> . . . the backlog was occasioned by the refusal of three stubborn old men not to retire. They retained their positions without functioning, without ever going into court, with the result that the only people who ever tried cases were visiting judges. These three old men hung on to the bitter end because they did not want to see a Democratic President fill the vacancies that would be created by their resignation.
>
> —Rep. Francis E. Walter (D–PA)

Our initial investigation of the federal judiciary is a broad-brush overview of the institution from 1869 to 1992. The inquiry is launched at 1869 because the permanent complement of circuit judges dates from the Reconstruction era,[1] so continuous examination of the lower federal bench as one entity is possible from then onward. Further, a stable, two-party system took root, one characterized by cyclical alternation in control of the executive branch under the Republicans from 1869–1932, the Democrats from 1933–68, and the Republicans again from 1969–92. Given the historically very high percentage of partisan appointments to the federal courts,[2] these cycles are useful for analyzing how swings in party dominance affect the composition of the bench. The balance of power in Congress and, by extension, whether government is unified under one party or not, is no less important to understanding federal court restructuring and the authorization of additional judgeships from 1869 to 1992.[3] Indeed, under conditions of unified government the membership of the courts can be rapidly and sizably augmented, whereas during times of split control the pace of altering bench size—if it occurs at all—is much slower.

The Justice Department, formed in 1870, and the Judicial Conference of the United States, chartered in 1922, also became active participants, along with the Senate of course, in recruiting the lower bench and coordinating its growth.[4] Also in 1922, Congress experimented with an omnibus legislative format for allocating additional judgeships. The Judicial Conference was charged with initiating the process.[5] Eighty percent of all currently authorized (through 1992) judgeships would be created over the ensuing 68 years,[6] mostly through these measures, and all administrations could anticipate receiving at least one such bill.

Filling vacancies arising from turnover is another important means for transforming the bench. Fed by the alluring retirement packages legislated by Congress, replacement appointments leapfrogged in importance with the mushrooming of bench size from 1869 to 1992. Beginning in 1869, federal judges, upon reaching the age of 70, could elect to retire with full pay after a stipulated period of continuous service. Moreover, those taking senior status could retire yet continue to hear cases on a part-time basis and still be eligible for all raises and benefits received by their full-time colleagues. Senior service proved to be irresistible. During Grant's administration, for example, fewer than 20 judges voluntarily left the bench, a number that ballooned to nearly 200 by the time Ronald Reagan left office. Typically the departures took place under a president of the judges' party, thereby facilitating partisan transformation of the third branch.[7] Over time, replacing voluntary leavers would become the chief means of staffing the courts.

The advent of circuit judges in 1869 and the creation of the U.S. Courts of Appeals some two decades later (1891) provided yet another avenue for placing same-party members on the bench, namely, elevations. Presidents could now consider advancing judges from one court level to the next, filling the ensuing vacancy, and thereby doubling the number of appointments.

The combination of new positions and swelling numbers of vacancies, owing especially to retirements, enabled modern presidents to change anywhere from 35 to 60 percent of the membership on the lower federal courts during their stay in office. Further, with 9 out of every 10 appointees sharing the partisan attachment of the chief executive, and with rotations in party control of the White House, gargantuan swings in the political composition of the bench became commonplace. Same-party control of the third branch by the second, then, is virtually axiomatic. Simply put: the contemporary federal judiciary is subject to massive alterations in its membership lists and numbers, features far removed from the intentions of the Federalists some two centuries ago who, in the Judiciary Act of 1789, thought they created a stable institution of limited size that through life tenure would be removed from the political pressures and passions of the day. The structure of the lower federal courts, along with the modern mechanisms of judicial staffing, then, took hold during the initial period of Republican hegemony.

In the analyses to follow, district and appellate judges are aggregated into one institution, the lower federal bench. This approach is valid, provided that

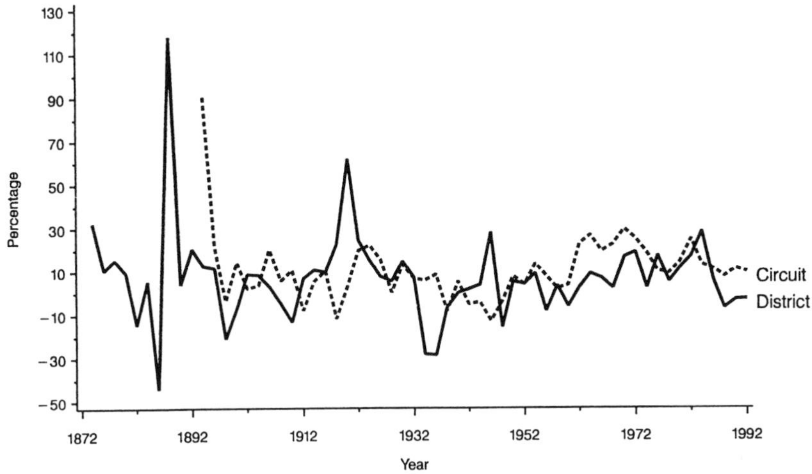

Fig. 2.1. Caseload change by level, 1872–1992

the patterns for the respective levels approximate each other.[8] Indeed, as we show, almost invariably the trends for the two are strikingly similar.[9] One area where such differences might be expected is in court business or case filings. Yet when the biennial percent change[10] in the number of filings for each level is plotted (see fig. 2.1), we see that the figures usually move in tandem. On only two occasions is there significant divergence: the increase in district court business during Prohibition and the drop in such filings in the aftermath of the 1929 stock market crash. Even when appellate filings surged during the 1960s, caseload on the district courts tracked along with them.

Such interlevel comity is important for several reasons. If historical trends are similar, then we can be confident that composite indicators are unfettered by tendencies peculiar to one court or the other. Accordingly, any discerned patterns become all the more significant for understanding institutional change. Commonalities across levels, then, encourage treatment of the lower federal bench as a single entity here, and perhaps in future research. Indeed, in many important respects the two courts evolved in similar ways, implying that federal judges in their professional and institutional perspectives are more alike than the difference in their functions might suggest.

The Federal Judiciary Database

The database used in this study is perhaps the most extensive and reliable of its kind. The unit of observation is an appointment, so there are second records for judges elevated to higher courts or positions.[11] The following information is coded for each appointee: name; month and year of appointment; date of birth and death; political party; appointing president; level of court; district (for district judges in multiple-district states); state; circuit; type of appointment (new seat or replacement)[12] and whether it took the form of an elevation or not, and, if so, the president who appointed the judge to the district bench; the appointee's predecessor (if a replacement position); party affiliation of home-state senators and control of government (unified vs. divided) at time of appointment; and month and year of and reason for leaving (death, retirement, resignation, elevation, failed confirmation, impeachment, termination of position, transfer). These data, in turn, can be combined in numerous ways. The party affiliations of the appointing president and appointee, for example, can be compared to determine if the latter was of the same party as the president or not (i.e., cross-party). Characteristics of appointees (e.g., party) can be matched with those of their predecessors, and positional histories can be traced, complementing those constructed for the U.S. Supreme Court.[13]

We have virtually complete information on the 2,514 judges appointed from 1869 to 1992,[14] and the 1,821 who left.[15] We were able to verify the party affiliation of all but 8 judges, for example; for a number of variables (e.g., dates of appointment and leaving, appointing president, reason for leaving) there are no missing cases. The intent was to construct a database that would be distinctive by its breadth, reliability, access and utilization, and capability of annual updating.

We came to realize that secondary sources are prone to inaccuracy, and often conflict with one another. Consequently the data are drawn primarily from government documents of varying scope and content, and then verified and cross-referenced. The data collection protocols and a description of the major sources used are appended to this chapter.

A Profile of the Life Cycle of the Lower Federal Courts

Appointments

Over the 1869–1992 span of the modern court system the preponderance (77.5 percent) of all appointments were made, of course, to the district courts. Perhaps more interesting is the distinctly Republican face of the bench—measured either as the percentage appointed by Republican presidents (see table 2.1) or as the proportion of judges affiliated with the GOP (see fig. 2.2).[16] Republican presidents made 60.3 percent of all appointments, attaining peak levels in the first (80.2 percent) and the third (76.4 percent) subperiods of GOP hold on the Oval Office and reaching a nadir (22.4 percent) in the middle era of Democratic Party control. The subperiod appointment patterns for Democrats, of course, are the reciprocals of the ones above. When party affiliation of the judges is considered, we find 58.2 percent Republicans, 40.9 percent Democrats, a scattering of Independents, and one Progressive.[17]

The data confirm the obvious—presidents overwhelmingly select members of their own party for federal judgeships. Indeed the partisan appointment rate, segmented by both party of the appointing president and level of court, are very similar, as they are across subperiods (93.5 percent, 94.3 percent, and 92.2 percent, respectively).[18] Given the near universal tendency to commission same-party jurists (93.2 percent), the interesting question is which circumstances prompt presidents to choose members of the opposition? Generally cross-party appointments are more likely to be made when presidents are politically vulnerable, such as when their party does not control the Senate, which of course must confirm nominees. Additionally, a president might suffer from low public esteem,[19] either throughout the entire administration (e.g., Ford) or during certain stages, usually at the end (e.g., Hoover,

TABLE 2.1. Appointment Patterns, 1869–1992

		Appointing President	
Variable	Overall	Republican	Democrat
All appointments	100%	60.3%	39.7%
District	77.5	60.6	39.4
Circuit	22.5	59.1	40.9
Same-party appointment rate	93.2	93.0	93.5
District	93.5	93.1	94.1
Circuit	92.2	92.6	91.6
New seats/all appointments	32.2	27.3	39.4
District	32.5	28.0	39.5
Circuit	30.8	25.1	38.9
Replacements/all appointments	67.8	72.6	60.6
District	67.4	72.0	60.4
Circuit	69.2	74.9	61.1
Elevation rate[a]	43.7	50.0	34.5
Age at time of appointment	50.0	50.0	51.0
District	50.0	49.0	50.0
Circuit	53.0	53.0	53.0
Age at time of elevation	55.0	55.0	55.0

	Party of the Judge		
	Republican	Democrat	Independent
Overall	58.2%	40.9%	0.9%
District[b]	58.5	40.7	0.8
Circuit	57.2	41.7	1.1

[a]All circuit court appointments.
[b]One district judge was affiliated with the Progressive Party.

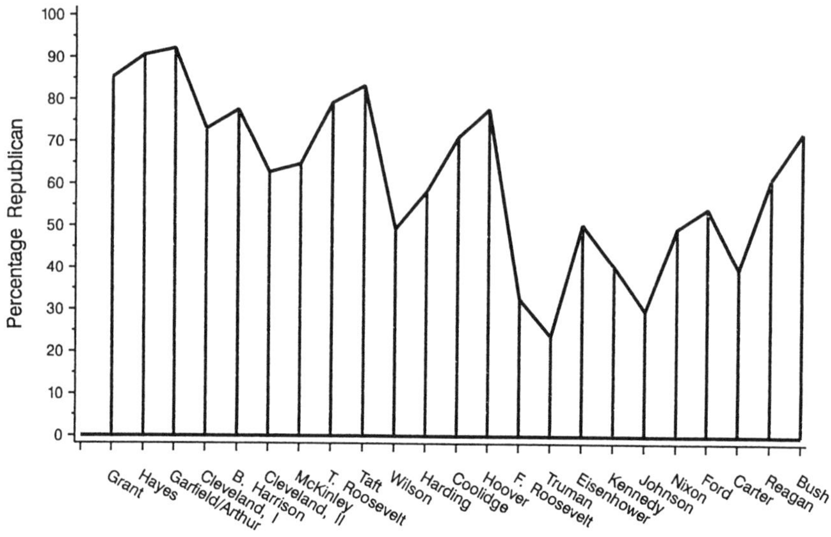

Fig. 2.2. Republican control of the bench, 1869–1992

Truman, Nixon), and the poor image can serve to diminish the frequency of partisan appointments. The converse is also true, as the inflated same-party appointment totals of FDR and Ronald Reagan show, especially early in their first terms. The president's political standing, then, apparently influences the inclination to make concessions to the opposition.

We also anticipate that such appointments are influenced by the political affiliation of the senators of the states to which the judges are appointed. Accordingly, we explore in later chapters the connection between the two during times when the president's party governs Congress, and otherwise. Relatedly, Evan A. Evans,[20] a student of the appointment process and a federal appellate judge, observed that when a party recaptures the White House after an extended absence—and with a bench stacked with judges of the other party—the opposition party will be more tolerant of presidential efforts to redress a politically imbalanced bench, at least up to a point. If so then we would expect higher partisan appointment rates in the early phases of Grover Cleveland's, FDR's, and Dwight Eisenhower's terms, for example.

Bench Expansion

At the close of the 40th Congress in 1868 there were 245 legislators and 52 lower court federal judges. A judiciary that in 1868 was 21 percent of the size of the first branch was 50 percent larger than it by 1992.[21] Historically, nearly one out of every three appointments is made to fill new seats (see table 2.1). Whereas there is little difference in the percentages of new seats by level of court (32.5 versus 30.8 percent), a sizable gulf separates the parties. The proportion of all appointments coming from new seats is 12 percentage points greater (at 39.4 percent), or 44 percent higher, for Democratic presidents. The reason for this disparity is the government control by Democrats since the 1930s. Most of the new judgeships were created by omnibus legislation commencing with the Act of 1922. From that point through the adjournment of the 102d Congress in 1992, Democrats ruled both houses of Congress for all but 20 years, or about 70 percent of the period. The major expansions in bench size, then, typically transpired during Democratic presidencies. Indeed, the allotment of new judgeships given to John F. Kennedy and Jimmy Carter, in particular, easily surpassed the number their immediate Republican predecessors garnered from their judgeship bills.

Figure 2.3 depicts the evolution in bench size from 1869 to 1992, segmented by administration. The proportion of all appointments going to new seats climbed steadily from 30 percent in the first period, to 31.4 percent in the middle period, and to 33.8 percent in the contemporary era.[22] Bench expansion is, of course, stimulated by increases in the business of the courts,

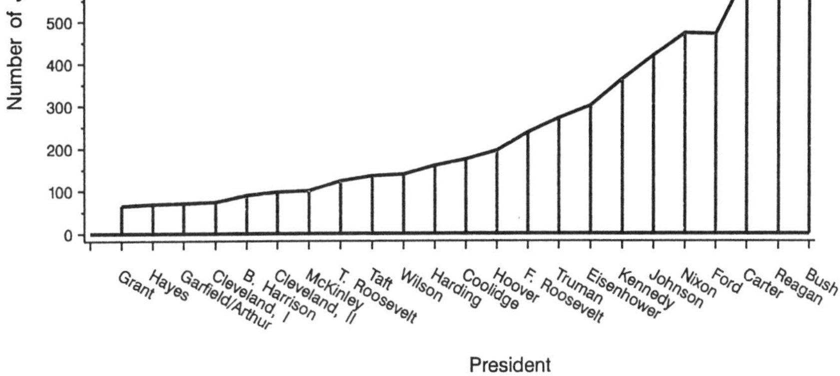

Fig. 2.3. Authorized judgeships, 1869–1992

in terms of both the amount (e.g., prohibition, bankruptcy) and complexity (e.g., civil rights, regulatory issues) of litigation. We expect that the timing and extent of institutional growth also depends upon political factors, notably whether government is unified under one party or not. Same-party control of both the House and the Senate is also a consideration in this matter as the creation of new seats and courts is a legislative power shared by both chambers, whereas confirmations of course devolve to the Senate alone.

Combining elements of cross-party appointments with the politics of bench expansion, we anticipate that these appointments will be greater for new seats than for postings to fill vacancies. The premise is that when the judicial "pie" is enlarged, the opposition party is able to assert a claim for at least a slice or two of the patronage.[23]

Departures

Age and Length of Service. With the aggrandizements in retirement packages, judges who resign generally do so to take positions elsewhere in government or in the more lucrative private sector. Accordingly, as table 2.2 indicates, resignees typically leave the bench at a significantly younger age (57 versus 70) and with fewer years of service (10 versus 17) than retirees. Mean years of service and age at departure are more or less the same when the resignation data are segmented by Republican and Democratic administrations or by party of the judge.[24]

There is significant variation by subperiod. A retirement option with pay was not established until 1869, and prior to 1919 the qualifications were ambiguous and benefits limited (see chap. 3). Resignation, then, was the primary way of voluntarily leaving the bench for much of the 1869–1932 era.[25] The mean age and length of service of those who resigned during these years was 59 and 11 years, respectively, compared to 74 and 19 for retirees. When retirement as the means of leaving took hold in the second subperiod, the average age of resigners fell to 57 and their tenure in office declined to 9 years. With the blossoming of retirement as the path of egress from the bench in the contemporary era, the typical judge who resigned did so at age 53 with 8 years of service.[26] Mean age at retirement likewise decreased from 74 in the first era, to 73 in the second, and to 69 in the third, whereas length of service held steady at 19 years in the first and middle subperiods, dropping to 16 in the third.[27]

Voluntary Departures. Table 2.2 details voluntary leaving patterns. We see that resignations play a rather modest role historically, comprising less than 10 percent of the total, and steadily declining from one era to the next with the advent of retirement and improvements in benefits. Whereas 37 percent of those leaving the bench voluntarily from 1869 to 1932 resigned, the

TABLE 2.2. Leaving Patterns, 1869–1992

Variable	Overall	Leaving President: Republican	Leaving President: Democrat
Resignations[a]	9.8%	9.9%	9.6%
District	9.5	10.1	8.1
Circuit	11.2	9.3	14.8
Retirements[a]	49.0	52.1	43.1
District	46.9	50.4	40.4
Circuit	56.3	58.3	52.6
Involuntary[a]	26.0	22.0	33.5
District	25.9	21.2	34.8
Circuit	26.5	25.1	28.9
Voluntary leaving rate[b]	53.7	61.4	41.9
District	54.1	61.9	41.8
Circuit	52.6	59.7	42.8
Involuntary leaving rate[c]	18.9	17.4	21.2
District	18.9	16.7	22.3
Circuit	18.9	20.0	17.3
Same-party leaving rate[d]	55.7	52.4	63.3
District	54.9	51.4	63.5
Circuit	57.9	55.4	62.6
Mean age at leaving—resigners	57.0	57.0	57.0
District	56.0	57.0	56.0
Circuit	59.0	61.0	57.0
Mean age at leaving—retirees	70.0	69.0	71.0
District	70.0	69.0	71.0
Circuit	71.0	70.0	72.0
Mean years served—resigners	10.0	10.0	10.0
District	10.0	10.0	10.0
Circuit	10.0	11.0	8.0
Mean years served—retirees	17.0	16.0	18.0
District	18.0	17.0	18.0
Circuit	16.0	15.0	16.0

[a] *N* of pertinent category/all leavers.
[b] Resigned + retired + elevated/all appointments.
[c] Involuntary departures (death, impeachment, position abolished)/all appointments.
[d] Same-party leavers (resigners and retirees)/all resigners and retirees.

figure plummets to 8.4 percent in the second period and to only 7.7 percent in the third. Interlevel differences are inconsequential. Retirements, by contrast, comprise about two-thirds of all voluntary turnover, ranging from 29 percent in the first era to 70 percent in the second, and to 77 percent in the third.[28]

Retirements—like appointments—take on a partisan cast, with Republican percentages noticeably higher. Nearly 70 percent of all retirees left during Republican presidencies. Breaking the figures down by level of court does not change the equation: 70.2 percent of all retirements on the district courts and 67.7 percent on the appellate bench occurred when a Republican sat in the White House. The same holds true of resignations and elevations.[29] These differences are to be expected. After all, Republicans occupied the Oval Office more than 60 percent of the time from 1869–1992, and so the odds favored leaving under a GOP administration.

Although one out of every five of the judges died in office, the myth of "hold[ing] their offices during good behaviour [*sic*]" (tenure for life; Article III, Section 1) is certainly dispelled in the modern era. Deaths in office, accounting for one-third of all appointment opportunities in the first subperiod, declined to 23 percent in the second and 8.7 percent in the last. There is no significant variation by level of court. Whereas this form of involuntary turnover tends to be somewhat higher during Democratic administrations, the interparty differences narrowed substantially from more than 20 percentage points in the first era to less than 2 in the third. A more subtle explanation for this divergence rests on the notion of party control. With Republicans dominating the executive branch in the first and third eras and Democrats in the second, and with judges tending to retire during a same-party administration to enable a partisan replacement, we would expect to see length of service and even death-in-office rates to be higher for judges affiliated with the opposition party in these eras as they extend their stay on the bench (perhaps until death), awaiting the election of a president from their party.

Voluntary Turnover and Appointments. The percentage of all appointments emanating from vacancies created by resignations, retirements, and elevations is 53.7 percent. Only 41.9 percent in the first subperiod, the figure rises to 64.1 percent in the contemporary era, proving to be the most significant source of appointment opportunities.[30] The partisan leaving rate—like the voluntary and involuntary turnover percentages—varies by party, except in this instance the numbers are more than 10 percentage points higher during Democratic administrations (63.3 to 52.4 percent). To understand why, we explore the leaving tendencies of judges under differing administrations and political conditions. Whereas partisan turnover rates were inordinately low during Democratic administrations in the first subperiod, those in the contemporary era (Kennedy, Johnson, Carter) are among some of the highest this century.[31] These presidents benefited, of course, from the growing cohort of Democratic jurists commissioned by virtue of the omnibus judgeship bills of the Roosevelt and Truman years who, now that a Democrat was in office, were ready to retire. As detailed in chapter 5 (see also figure 2.4), there is in fact a generational pattern to replacement appointments among Democrats in the third era: Roosevelt and Truman appointees typically left the bench under Kennedy and Johnson, whose own appointees departed under Carter.

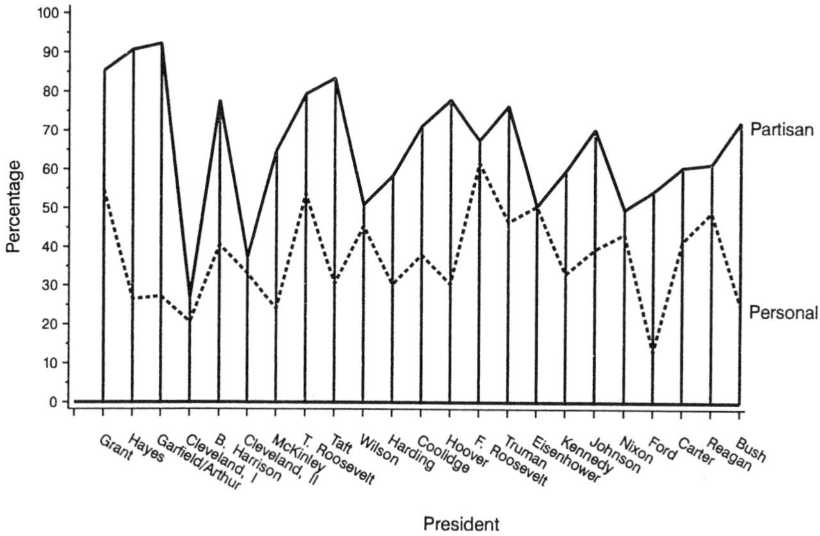

Fig. 2.4. Cohorts on the bench at leaving, 1869–1992

The opportunity to depart during a same-party presidency is very much a function of secular political realities. Assuming that voluntary leavers try to time their departures politically,[32] then these judges are by definition relatively advanced in age, so to execute the feat there must be a compatriot in the White House. The lowest partisan turnover rate in the first era (and in the span of the data) occurred in Grover Cleveland's first administration (20 percent). The obvious explanation is that the term of the 23d president was preceded by 24 successive years of Republican occupancy of the White House and the Civil War, so there were only a handful of active Democratic judges in the first place.[33] The next lowest rate (35 percent) came during Franklin Roosevelt's tenure, he being only the third Democrat to serve in the wake of 72 years of almost uninterrupted Republican control of the White House. Excepting Ford's abbreviated term in office, Eisenhower heads the Republican list (47.4 percent), and for the same reason: his presidency came on the heels of two decades of Democratic control of the Oval Office and, by extension, control of the third branch (see fig. 2.2).

We expect that the appointment opportunities afforded presidents will increasingly devolve from voluntary departures, courtesy of the senior status option created by Congress. Second, we anticipate that judges will try to time their departures politically, that is, retire under presidents sharing their party attachment. Same-party leaving should accelerate, then, when government is unified, given that judges are cognizant of the president nominating replacements to a politically compatible Senate. Conversely, cross-party leavers should be older, on the premise that they endeavor to delay retirement in the hope that a member of their party will capture the White House.

Elevations

The elevation rate for all administrations from 1869 to 1992 is 43.7 percent.[34] Breaking the data down by party of the president, the rate for Republicans is 50.0 percent compared to only 34.5 percent for Democrats. Indeed, 11 of the 15 Republican administrations under study registered percentages above the norm for their party (see fig. 2.5)[35] whereas only two Democrats (Cleveland in his second term and Johnson) exceeded the historical average. Party alone can not explain the wide discrepancy; the size of the pool of compatible district court judges needs to be taken into account. If the ranks of this group are small or nil, then presidents obviously will be less inclined to elevate, opting instead to appoint from outside the bench. Note for instance that, excepting Grant's term when the office of circuit judge was in its infancy, the lowest percentages among Republicans occurred during Eisenhower's presidency, which was preceded, of course, by a 20-year Democratic hold on the

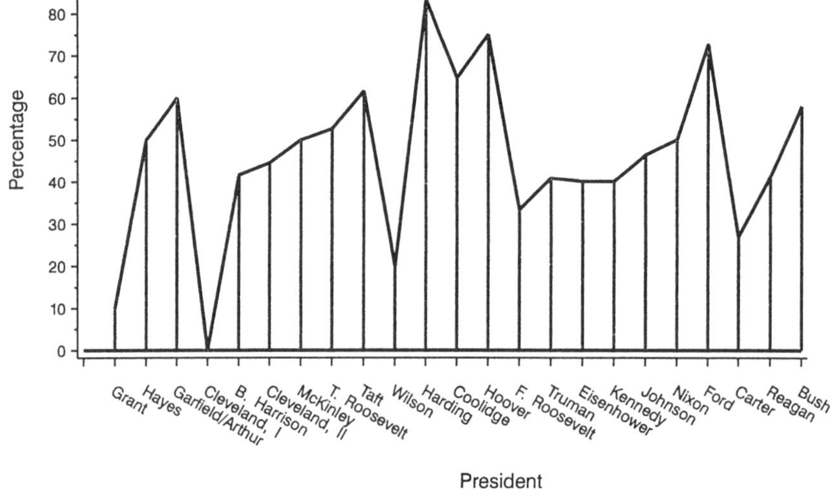

Fig. 2.5. Elevation rate, 1869–1992

White House and a corresponding winnowing of Republican numbers on the bench. A similar situation faced Grover Cleveland and Woodrow Wilson in the first era with equal effect.[36]

Realizing that elevations maximize appointment opportunities, we expect the practice to be common yet constrained by the partisan composition of the district judge pool. Government control (of the Senate) also enters the equation. Following the premise that divided government induces a president to make concessions to the opposition party in the form of cross-party appointments, we expect that elevations will increase under such conditions.

Institutional Change

Whereas only a few presidents (e.g., Franklin Roosevelt, Ronald Reagan) are considered "court-packers," almost all were able to stack the court with partisans—in some cases in very short order. Among 23 presidents, only Grover Cleveland, who twice served in an extraordinarily Republican-dominated era, and Richard Nixon failed to leave the White House with the judiciary in their party's hands.[37] Nixon, nevertheless, came within a percentage point of realizing the feat, which is all the more remarkable considering the Watergate debacle. Conversely, Woodrow Wilson and Dwight Eisenhower, among others, transmuted sizable—and in the case of the former, daunting—opposite party majorities by the time they left office. Moreover, in only six instances did a president's cohort on the courts comprise less than 30 percent at the close of their administration.[38] Ten attained a percentage of 40 percent or more, and three of over 50 percent (see fig. 2.4).[39] Reagan, parenthetically, is not among this latter group.

Conclusion

The historical data chronicle an institution doubling in size every three decades and subject to ever-growing rates of turnover, largely through retirements. These twin conditions, in turn, permitted most presidents to recompose the bench within the life of their administration. This overview establishes the importance of structural and political factors in the evolution of the federal judiciary. An analysis of subperiods is undertaken next to explore the ways in which the institution conforms to or departs from the benchmarks staked here under the varying conditions of unified and divided government, and during alternating periods of Republican and Democratic control of the executive branch. The ability to remake the courts is naturally a function of how long a president or party retains power. A tempering or intervening condition is government control. When government is divided, for instance, bench growth should be limited, with appointment opportunities from voluntary departures or elevations becoming more prevalent. When the president's party comprises a majority in Congress, however, transformation of the courts should come primarily from the creation of new judgeships.

The data presented in this and the next three chapters trace the expansion of the lower federal courts from fewer than 50 district courts and a roughly equal number of judges in 1869 to more than 100 courts staffed by over 800 jurists today. We pay special attention to the role omnibus judgeship legislation played in this regard, outlining the politics of bench growth and the intriguing interplay between the Judicial Conference of the United States, the policy-making arm of the third branch, the Congress, which ultimately determines the timing and extent of membership change, and the Oval Office, ever eager to cast the courts in its own partisan image. We detail how the mix of new positions and turnover shaped partisan appointments and presidential cohorts on the courts. As another sounding of the stability of the institutions, length of service statistics are explored to determine whether the old and noble notion of lifetime service has changed in recent times.

APPENDIX

A wide variety of sources were used to compile the data used in this study. Because each is limited, it was important to determine the superior reference for each particular type of information. Cross-referencing was critical to detecting and resolving conflicting or inaccurate information. Our familiarity with a vast number of works enabled us to discern the strengths and weaknesses of each, and so we developed a "schedule of confidence" among the different sources. We generally relied on government documents or otherwise consulted *Judges of the United States*[40] because it is based on primary data solicited through surveys of the judges (or family members when the individual is deceased) and extensive information from the U.S. archives. Third in order is the *Federal Reporter.*[41] Although not a government document per se it is an official reporter receiving its information directly from court officials. The fourth ranked source is *Federal Cases,*[42] useful as a check on historical data because it is based on extensive contacts with surviving family members and judicial colleagues of each judge listed. Finally, there is an assortment of directories and other secondary material described below.

Data Sources

The following sources helped us to identify judges and to determine their courts, appointing president, length of service, and other aspects of their careers. Drawing on numerous primary (federal government) and secondary sources we pinpointed the date of and the reason for the appointment and the departure of every judge. Most of the exiting information came from the *Journal of the Executive Proceedings of the Senate of the United States of America.*[43] When the data were unavailable from these volumes or when we otherwise wanted to supplement or cross-reference, the following sources were helpful: *Legislative History of the United States Courts of Appeals and the Judges Who Served During the Period 1801 Through May 1972,*[44] *Federal Cases, Federal Reporter, Legislative and Executive Calendar of the U.S. Senate Committee on the Judiciary,*[45] various reports of the Congressional Research Service,[46] *Biographical Dictionary of the Federal Judiciary,*[47] and *The Third Branch.*[48]

A variety of sources were used to compile background information. Each has particular virtues and drawbacks. *Judges of the United States* was especially valuable for its historical (1789–1981) data on appointing president, location of court, political party, commission and elevation dates. The same source also listed, if known, the place and date of birth, death and interment, and the educational and employment history of each judge. This definitive reference does not, however, provide information on type of appointment (replacement or new seat, and the predecessor if the former), recess appointments, and exiting. It also has a 1981 cutoff date, and for some reason omits a number of Carter appointees. Chase, et al.,[49] for many years the standard reference on the federal judiciary, has a number of limitations and was used sparingly. It does provide some information on turnover during the period 1789–1975, making it a useful complement to *Judges of the United States.*

The authoritative references on appointments are the *Register of the Department of Justice and the Courts of the United States*[50] and the *Journal of the Executive Proceedings of the Senate of the United States of America.*[51] *Legislative History of the Courts of Appeals and the Judges Who Served During the Period 1801 through May 1972*[52] contains a variety of hard-to-come-by background information on members of the courts of appeals. Edwin Surrency's work[53] is valuable for its information on judges appointed to the district courts, dates of commission, length of service, and judgeship legislation. *The American Bench,*[54] a biographical series first published in 1977 and now in its fifth volume, indexes appellate judges alphabetically, and the others by state. Scholars will find it useful because it is updated every two to four years, and the serial reports a variety of important biographical data on each judge. *The American Bench,* however, contains information on only those either in active service or holding senior status at the time of publication. Moreover, the information on recently appointed judges, based as it is on the latter's response (or lack of one) to questionnaires sent to them by the publisher, often is sketchy.

The *Federal Judiciary Almanac,*[55] which is no longer being published, follows the format of *The American Bench,* and occasionally contains information not available in the latter. The *Judicial Staff Directory*[56] likewise provides biographical data on active and senior status judges, and from time to time has information about a particular judge that the others do not. *The Almanac of the Federal Judiciary,*[57] like *The American Bench* and *Judicial Staff Directory,* focuses on active/senior status judges and helps to extend the domain of what we know about the federal judiciary. *Federal Cases* is useful for its biographical information on federal judges who served during the period 1789–1893. It is especially useful for its exiting information. *Who's Who in America, Who Was Who in America, Who's Who in American Law, Who's Who in American Politics,*[58] and their various editions, *Dictionary of American Biography,*[59] *The National Cyclopedia of American Biography,*[60] *Biographical Directory of the*

United States Executive Branch,[61] and *Biographical Directory of the United States Congress, 1774–1989*[62] round out the secondary source biographical portraits of the federal judiciary.

Our data collection efforts were facilitated enormously by the cooperation of several government agencies and officials, most notably the staffs of the Senate Judiciary Committee (formerly chaired by Joseph Biden, D–DE), the Senate Judiciary Subcommittee on Courts and Administrative Practice (formerly chaired by Howell Heflin, D–AL), and the Federal Judicial Center, which is in the process of producing a third edition of *Judges of the United States*.

CHAPTER 3

Molding the Court in Their Own Image: The First Republican Hegemony

> If this [Judicial] Conference is created it will be recommending more judgeships as long as the Republic lasts. The recommendations, where frequently their own interests are involved, will be presented here as having the weight of official character. For the sake of the good name of our Federal judiciary we can not afford to put it in a position of such self seeking.
>
> —Rep. Clarence Lea (D–CA)

Ulysses Grant's election in 1868 inaugurated an unprecedented period in American politics. The Grand Old Party, formed in only 1854, triumphed in all but 4 of the next 16 presidential contests, enjoying control of government in 17 out of 32 congresses.[1] Never before or since has one party dominated the legislative and executive machinery of government for so long, a factor crucial to evaluating the transformation of the lower federal courts during the era.

Like the High Court, the lower federal judiciary remained largely unchanged from its inception in 1789 through the early years of Reconstruction. The institution, however, was to be profoundly and permanently altered by legislation and by politics over the next 64 years. Two important signposts of the change were the marked increase in additional positions and the extent of court restructuring, transformations that are striking when compared to the early years of these courts.

We see in figure 3.1 that at the end of the Federalist era in 1801, for example, there were 20 judgeships for the entire lower bench, excluding the recently terminated positions on the First through Sixth Circuits.[2] Three were on the Circuit Court for the District of Columbia, with the remainder on the district courts. The total reached 28 at the beginning of Andrew Jackson's presidency, climbing to 52 by the conclusion of Andrew Johnson's tenure in office.[3] Only district court judges were in service at this time, representing 49 judicial districts including the District of Columbia.[4] Thus, the size of the bench barely doubled from 1801 to 1868. It doubled again by the turn of the century, and nearly did so once more by the time Herbert Hoover left office. There were by then 181 permanent positions,[5] distributed over 11 courts of appeals and 86 judicial districts.[6]

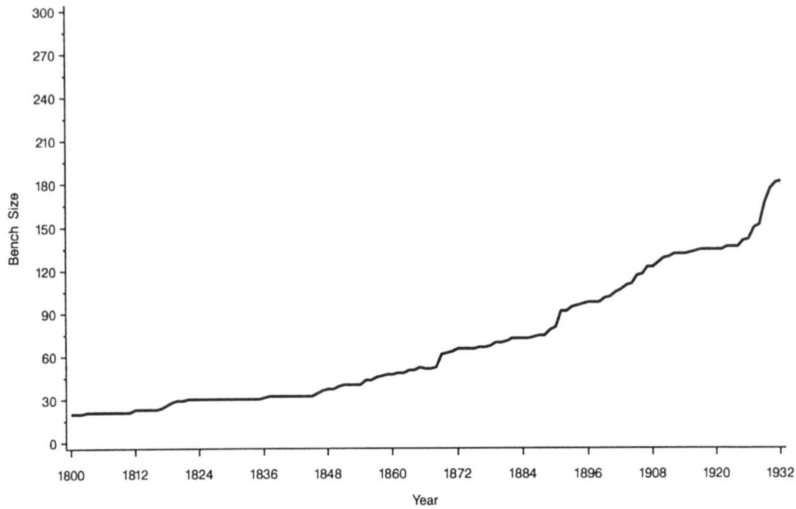

Fig. 3.1. Growth of the federal bench, 1801–1932

The scope as well as the scale of appointments rose dramatically during the first subperiod. Presidents, of course, overwhelmingly stock the courts with members of their own political party (see chap. 2), be they Federalists, Whigs, Democrats, or Republicans.[7] Yet the sheer increase in the number of judicial offices and the extension of the federal court system to 48 states and the District of Columbia,[8] coupled with the growth in voluntary turnover by federal judges through resignation, retirement, or elevation led to a degree of institutional change from 1869–1932 unthinkable to Grant's predecessors.

Indeed, Presidents Washington through Johnson commissioned slightly under 200 federal judges (see table 3.1). Grant alone put one-fifth of that total on the bench during his two terms (see table 3.2). Moreover, at the close of his

TABLE 3.1. Sources of Appointments to the Lower Federal Courts, 1789–1868 and 1869–1932 (by positions filled)

	1789–1868	1869–1932
New seats	29.7%[a]	28.9%
Elevations	4.2	13.8
Voluntary turnover replacements	23.4	26.2
Involuntary turnover replacements	42.7	31.1
Total	192.0	595.0

[a]Excludes appointments to the first through sixth Judicial Circuits.

TABLE 3.2. Appointments to the Lower Federal Courts, 1869–1932 (by positions filled)

Administration	Unified Government	New Positions	Elevations	Voluntary Turnover Replacements	Involuntary Turnover Replacements	Total Appointments
Grant	75%	36.7%	2.4%	39.0%	22.0%	41
Hayes	0	15.0	10.0	15.0	60.0	20
Garfield/Arthur	50	14.3	23.8	42.9	19.0	21
Cleveland I	0	20.0	0.0	40.0	40.0	15
Harrison	50	39.5	18.4	18.4	23.7	38
Cleveland II	50	26.9	15.4	15.4	42.3	26
McKinley	100	29.4	11.8	32.4	26.5	34
T. Roosevelt	100	27.4	17.8	32.9	21.9	73
Taft	50	20.0	14.3	12.9	52.9	70
Wilson	75	13.7	8.2	35.6	42.5	73
Harding	100	46.8	12.8	17.0	23.4	47
Coolidge	100	31.2	14.3	22.1	32.5	77
Hoover	50	43.3	21.7	26.6	8.3	60

administration not only was the bench about 85 percent Republican (see table 3.3), but nearly two out of every three (64 percent) were appointees of the 18th president, posted to 21 of the 37 states and the District of Columbia. The proportion and geographical breadth of Grant's appointments presaged court staffing trends common ever since.

The increase in bench size and pace of court restructuring resulted in part from granting statehood to 11 western territories. These additions spawned 13 new judicial districts and two circuits.[9] The proliferation of new positions, however, came primarily in response to the explosive rise in caseload, not to mention the increasing complexity of legal issues on both the appellate and district courts. The number of filings on the latter, for instance, skyrocketed from about 25,000 cases per year in 1870 to more than 150,000 by 1932. The filing rate in the courts of appeals likewise ballooned from 840 in 1892, the inaugural year, to 6,170 forty years later.[10]

Responding to the caseload crunch, Congress steadily increased the number and type of judges, especially on the federal circuits, where justices of the Supreme Court of the United States long had bemoaned the onerous task of "riding circuit." Beginning with an initial allocation of 9 circuit judges by the Act of April 10, 1869,[11] this cadre grew to 45 by 1932. The additional work force significantly reduced the High Court's caseload. Indeed, in a three year period alone from 1890 (one year before a second wave of additional appellate judgeships was created) through 1892 (one year after the event), the number of such cases fell by 56 percent.[12]

TABLE 3.3. Partisan and Institutional Change on the Lower Federal Courts, 1869–1932

Administration	Partisan Appointment Rate	Partisan Proportion on the Bench (swing)	Presidential Cohort
Grant	95.5%	85.2% (+26.1)	64.1%
Hayes	90.0	90.6 (+5.4)	27.9
Garfield/Arthur	91.5	92.2 (+1.6)	30.0
Cleveland I	100.0	26.9 (+19.1)	24.7
Harrison	92.1	77.6 (+4.5)	41.6
Cleveland II	100.0	37.2 (+14.8)	27.8
McKinley	91.2	64.6 (+1.8)	34.0
T. Roosevelt	91.9	79.3 (+14.7)	61.0
Taft	85.4	83.3 (+4.0)	40.0
Wilson	98.6	50.7 (+34.0)	53.2
Harding	97.9	58.2 (+8.9)	30.8
Coolidge	91.1	71.1 (+12.9)	46.6
Hoover	85.0	77.8 (+6.7)	37.4

Reform came as well with the newly formed Department of Justice in 1870, charged with, among other matters, collecting, maintaining, and reporting information on the federal courts such as caseload, conducting background checks on nominees, and publishing a register of the judges. The Department of Justice came to play a crucial role in the evolution toward centralization of judicial administration generally and especially in the recruitment and selection of federal judges. Indeed the attorney general often took the lead in encouraging members of Congress to introduce judgeship bills; the department, in turn, provided supporting data.[13] Momentum for coordinating staffing and bench growth, then, was building.

Bench Expansion: The Rules of the Game Change

The dockets of district judges, who often heard circuit court cases, also were lightened by the influx of new judges in 1869 (see fig. 3.1). Relief—albeit sporadic—came as well from the creation of multiple districts in some states and additional judgeships in virtually all judicial districts.[14] Not until the Act of September 14, 1922, however, would routine and systematic changes and additional positions be brought to these courts.[15] This landmark legislation authorized 24 new district court judgeships, a record number. Henceforth every administration could anticipate omnibus increases in personnel.[16]

No less important, the 1922 act established the Judicial Conference of the United States to review and to submit annual reports to Congress on recommended changes. Former president and appellate judge and then Chief Justice Taft zealously advocated this type of organization to no avail during Woodrow Wilson's presidency.[17] He also championed creation of a core of "roving" judges based in one district or circuit, but available for temporary assignment to another with an especially heavy caseload as a means of clearing clogged dockets. The five judges simultaneously appointed by Taft to the short-lived U.S. Commerce Court and to the courts of appeals under the Act of June 18, 1910 insinuated what he had in mind. Nevertheless, the idea of a permanent core of peripatetic judges got a cool reception on Capitol Hill and it was eventually dropped. Taft then focused on other ways of expanding the ranks of lower court judges.

The Republican return to power in 1921 and Taft's own appointment to the U.S. Supreme Court the same year gave him a new and better perch from which to press his cause.[18] Indeed, the new chief justice tirelessly promoted judicature reform on the floor and cloakrooms of Congress. Success came with the passage of the 1922 act and the formation of the Judicial Conference. Thus the act was a watershed for the institutional expansion of the federal bench for two reasons—it was the largest single increase in the complement of federal judges and it established a structure and a process for recommending new positions in which the judiciary itself was to play a lead role.

The backdrop to the act follows. By 1921 criminal court caseload had increased nearly 800 percent over what it was in 1912, owing largely to Prohibition legislation.[19] The Attorney General's Office asked for new judges to alleviate "congestion" in the courts,[20] and both Chief Justice Taft and the attorney general testified at the House Judiciary Committee hearings on the need for additional judges. Following an initial round of hearings, the two conferred with the chairs of each chamber's Judiciary Committee and examined caseload pressures in each judicial district, ultimately agreeing on a bill (H.R. 9103) providing for 23 new positions and several changes in the Judicial Code. Attention to the latter consumed the lion's share of time in both houses, and those portions of the debate inform the issue of the importance of unified government for the politics of judicial administration.[21]

H.R. 9103 called for the creation of the Judicial Conference of the United States as the chief administrative arm of the federal courts, to serve as an initiator in the process of institutional growth and perform a clearance function for coordinating proposals affecting the administration of the federal court system. Each year the senior circuit judges would survey the business of their appellate and district courts to determine whether there was a need for increased staffing. These judges or their representatives would then convene in Washington during the second week in September for the Judicial Conference, chaired by the chief justice. The attorney general could join in the discussions of court business, but was not a voting member. Judgeship needs would be assessed systemwide prior to making recommendations to the Congress, so that

> Instead of having occasional and disjointed and disconnected communications between the Chief Justice and the various circuit judges, we have provided for a meeting at which the requirements of all the districts can be considered and compared. . . . The needs can not be considered in their absolute sense. They must be considered in their comparative sense. A great many of the courts, at least when they give their account of the business pending before them, will indicate that they need additional force, but there must be a comparison of these necessities, so that the public welfare may be most certainly promoted.[22]

Democrats countered that the Conference machinery violated the principle of separation of powers by forcing the judiciary to intrude on Congress' prerogative to create "such inferior courts as the Congress may from time to time ordain and establish."[23] The consequence would be "the most serious assault that has ever been made upon the integrity and independence of the judiciary of the country,"[24] leading as well to judicial self-aggrandizement:

> . . . it [the bill] places the judiciary of the country in a self-seeking position . . . the conference proposed would easily deteriorate into a publicity-seeking propaganda effort. . . . We should not endanger the prestige of our judges or invite them into fields of destroying controversies by compelling them to perform functions primarily legislative or political. . . . This conference scheme will tend to organize our Federal judges into a judicial machine. It will furnish new grounds of attack by those who would weaken and destroy the functions of our Federal courts.[25]

Over the protests of Democrats, who apparently felt that they would receive little of the expected patronage emanating from this provision, the Judicial Conference machinery was virtually unchanged in the final version of the bill.[26]

Far less controversy surfaced over the judgeship part of the bill, especially considering that the amount of bench expansion called for was epic by historical standards. Essentially what the House resolution did was "bundle" 15 bills for individual new positions that were introduced in the prior Congress. The rub, at least for Democrats, was that these bills, introduced by Democrats at the eleventh hour of Wilson's presidency, argued for additional positions on the basis of a caseload crunch. Yet with the 66th Congress in Republican hands, the situation of divided government allowed GOP congressional leaders to block final action. In considering the new proposal, then, the Democrats were handcuffed by their own arguments. Indeed as Rep. William D. Boies (R–IA) put it:

> I am surprised that the opposition to this bill comes from the minority side of this Chamber. I do not forget that prior to the 4th day of last March there were several applications presented to the Committee on the Judiciary of this House by Democrats for additional Federal judges. Since that time the demand has been rather quiet from their standpoint.[27]

The debate and subsequent vote in both chambers closely followed party lines. Republicans focused their defense of the bill on caseload statistics, whereas Democrats tried to poke holes in those numbers and otherwise argue that, "Pie, judicial pie, is the moving power behind this bill."[28] Democrats claimed that the caseload statistics were misleading because the bulk of the criminal cases, for example, were Prohibition violations that probably would never come to trial. There was also a spate of draft violations from World War I that cluttered the dockets but would likely never be tried either. So, from their standpoint

> . . . statistics or generalizations . . . will not support the character of legislation now contended for, and that in the absence of full proof upon so grave and serious a matter you should not shock—and I use the language rather conservatively—the public conscience of the American people by increasing the number of judges from 105 to 127 in a few hours of debate. Beware of impairing or imperiling the American judiciary. Lift it above partisan consideration. We should look more for justice and less for judges.[29]

Democrats additionally leveled a litany of charges against the judiciary in general and certain judges in particular for not being sufficiently diligent or efficient in disposing of their dockets and therefore creating a backlog. Judge Kennesaw Mountain Landis of the Northern District of Illinois was the preferred target. Landis, a Republican and Roosevelt appointee, became the first Commissioner of Baseball on the heels of the "Black Sox" scandal, yet he still sat on the bench.[30] Democrats moaned that the judge had shirked his judicial duties, for which he received an annual stipend of $7,500, in favor of his baseball responsibilities, paying him, for the time, the princely sum of $50,000 each year.

Another tack was to admit there was legitimate need for some new positions, but to reject the packaging of a number of requests into one omnibus bill that would be voted up or down. Democrats, instead, fell back on the argument that requests for additional judgeships should be legislated one at a time:

> I say, Mr. President, let every tub stand on its own bottom. If a judge is needed in any district, let a Senator from that State introduce a bill, have it referred to the committee and let it be reported back to the Senate, and passed. But do not let us have a wholesale bill like this measure.[31]

Ironically, roles would be reversed in congressional deliberations of judgeship bills in the New Deal era, with the (minority) Republicans arguing to no avail that bench expansion should be considered on a position-by-position basis rather than in omnibus fashion.

After lengthy debate, the House passed its version of H.R. 9103, which provided for 22 new district judgeships, on December 11, 1921.[32] Almost four months later the Senate passed a similar version calling for 25 positions.[33] The conference committee produced a report in which the Senate receded from its differences with the House version in the changes in the Judicial Code and the House agreed to the three additional lines authorized by the Senate bill. The enrolled bill was sent to President Harding, who signed it on September 14, 1922.

The 1922 bill "benchmarked" a number of patterns. First, consideration of omnibus judgeship bills is an intensely partisan affair. The party that will have the opportunity to fill the positions endorses the bill, while its counterpart opposes. Second, the condition of unified government is fertile ground for institutional growth of the third branch. Judgeship bills are more likely to be enacted when this situation obtains, and there are likely to be increases over what the Judicial Conference recommends. In this case it recommended 22 additional lines and 25 were ultimately authorized. Third, the partisan dynamics are tempered by the patronage aspects of omnibus bills—regardless of party, legislators are more likely to vote for the bills if they include positions for their states.

The votes on the conference version by both the House and the Senate illustrate all of these tendencies. Eighty-five percent of those Republicans voting in the House favored the measure, whereas 89.8 percent of the Democrats opposed it. Party membership aside, of those representatives whose states were to receive a new position, 78.0 percent voted "yea," as compared to 44.4 percent otherwise. Combining both the partisan and patronage elements, not a single Democrat from a state not graced in the bill voted for it, whereas 23.1 percent getting positions endorsed the bill. The patronage pattern, hoisted on partisan shoulders, is seen in the Republican vote: 93.9 percent voting for the measure represented states in line for additional positions, compared to 70.2 percent who were not getting seats.

The same patterns held in the Senate, where partisan support for the bill was 90.0 percent among Republicans and 27.8 percent for Democrats. Seventy-nine percent of all supporters were to receive new seats, whereas 61.8 percent of those opposed were not. Fifty-seven percent of the Democrats from states slated for new judgeships endorsed the bill, whereas only 9.1 percent of those not getting additional seats did. Although H.R. 9103 enjoyed overwhelming GOP support, patronage colored the vote here as well—every senator receiving a position voted in favor, compared to 87.0 percent of those not in line for new slots.

Thus the initiative for shaping the structure of the third branch, and the working conditions and emoluments of its members, passed from the Congress to an elite group of federal judges, the first such recommendations coming in September 1923. Not surprisingly, handsome increases in salary, retirement benefits, and bench size were routinely called for in Conference reports.[34] Whether Congress went along with the recommendations was another matter that more often than not rested on political considerations, as we develop here and in the next two chapters. It is worth noting that more than a third of the total number of new, permanent judgeships created between 1869 and 1932 came during the decade following formation of the Judicial Conference.[35]

Indeed, Chief Justice Taft had no qualms over planning, if not plotting, for new judgeships. During preparation of the fourth annual *Report of the Judicial Conference,* for example, the judges of the Southern District of New York thought the chances of receiving additional positions for their district would be better if two rather than three new judgeships were requested. Drawing on his knowledge of how Congress worked, Taft thought otherwise: "If they [the introducers of the bill] ask for three, we can probably get one Democrat, and if you get one Democrat, you will get the bill through."[36] The chief justice was right on the mark. Three additional judgeships were authorized for the Southern District of New York by the Act of February 29, 1929, and one of the three went to a Democrat.

A host of institutional forces from all three branches of government, then, orchestrated the expansion of the federal bench from 1869–1932. This coordination and cooperation brought about unparalleled alteration in both the structure and the composition of an institution designed for stability through lifetime appointment and independence. These changes were legislated over the course of 13 administrations, 10 of these Republican. We see in table 3.4 that 44 of the 50 appellate judgeships created from 1869 to 1932[37] were legislated in years when the Republican Party held a majority of seats in Congress, compared to only two positions authorized by a Democratic Congress (the 53d). Ninety-two percent of the new appeals court judgeships, then,

TABLE 3.4. Unified Government and Bench Expansion, 1869–1932, Authorized New Positions

Circuit Administration	Congress: Unified	Congress: Divided
Republican	44	3
Democratic	2	1
Total	46	4

District Administration	Congress: Unified	Congress: Divided
Republican	106	4
Democratic	10	2
Total	116	6

were crafted by congresses controlled by the president's party.[38] The story was the same for new seats on the district courts. Ninety percent ($N = 106$) were created in years when the GOP controlled Congress, and 95 percent of the total came during periods of unified control.

Judicial Turnover and Appointment Politics

There was yet another source of concern for Democrats. A seemingly innocuous concluding section of the 1869 Judgeship Act[39] would profoundly influence the scale and rate of recruitment, once again to the benefit of Republicans. Judges with ten years continuous service henceforth could elect to leave the bench at age 70 and continue to receive a salary for the remainder of their lives. Subsequent changes in the legislation would vary the length of service and salary mix and, more importantly, establish senior status. Federal judges now had the opportunity to "resign" with full pay, and they were expected if not encouraged to exercise the option.[40]

Consequently, during this era vacancies from voluntary turnover became an increasingly important fount of appointment opportunities. We see in table 3.1, for instance, that 595 appointments were made from 1869 to 1932, a number more than three times the 1789 to 1868 tally. Collapsing the figures into four categories based on source (new seats, elevations, voluntary turnover, involuntary turnover) clearly shows the trend toward voluntary turnover replacements. Forty-three percent of the appointment opportunities in the years before the advent of retirement legislation came from filling vacancies occurring from the death or removal from office of a federal judge. The figure fell to 29 percent from 1869 to 1932, during which time 30 percent of the appointments were to new positions, 27 percent went to filling vacancies from retirements or resignations, and the remaining 14 percent were to replace judges advancing to higher courts or positions.[41] Two out of every five appointments to the lower federal courts from 1869 to 1932, then, came by way of replacing judges who either voluntarily left the bench or were elevated. Further, the number of such opportunities increased steadily. Sixty-six percent of the total number of retirements or resignations between 1869 and 1932, for example, occurred after 1900.

Elevations and Appointment Politics

We saw that nine circuit judgeships were created to relieve the appellate caseload crunch by the Act of April 10, 1869. Yet the legislation passed by the Republican-controlled 41st Congress enabled Ulysses Grant and his successors to make several appointments at once: to fill the new circuit positions, of course, and to replace district judges who were elevated. Thus, the 1869 act permitted compounding of lower court appointments, thereby accelerating the rate of institutional change. The increased possibilities of patronage were not lost on the Democrats, who united in the House to try to defeat the measure to no avail, the bill easily carrying by a vote of 90–53.[42]

The practice of elevating judges from one court level to another quickly took hold. Whereas only 10 percent of Grant's appointees to circuit judgeships took this route, Rutherford B. Hayes advanced half of the total he placed in these positions, and 60 percent of the appellate judges named by James Garfield and Chester Arthur were promoted from the district courts.[43] Democrat Grover Cleveland, Arthur's successor, in contrast, made no elevations his first term in office. The fact that he inherited a judiciary that was 92 percent Republican, the most lopsided balance on the lower federal courts since the Federalist years, explains why none of Cleveland's circuit court judges were drawn from these ranks.[44] The situation changed, however, in his second term. With the Democratic pool on the district courts now adequate if not plentiful, elevations figured in 56 percent of Cleveland's appointments to appellate judgeships.

Benjamin Harrison, Cleveland's Republican successor, was given a fresh cache of appellate court judgeships to fill,[45] courtesy of the 51st Congress under his party's control, as well as the opportunity to fill several vacancies. Just under half (45 percent) of Harrison's cohort on these courts were elevated. Thirty years passed before Congress authorized another parcel of these judgeships. The context remained the same, however: government was unified under the Republicans. The beneficiary of the Act of June 18, 1910 was President Taft, who used elevations to secure over 60 percent of his placements on the courts of appeals. The final restructuring of the appellate bench during the era came on February 28, 1929, with the division of the Eighth Circuit to create a new Tenth Circuit. The additional positions legislated by the 70th Congress[46] went to President Hoover, who, in turn, parlayed 16 appointments into 26 by elevating over half (63 percent) of the total placed on these courts.

Caseload statistics notwithstanding, the timing of the legislation authorizing appeals court judgeships in the first place, and the political conditions present when such positions were created, advantaged Republican presidents. Looking at such one-sided numbers conveys the magnitude of the staffing problem confronting Democrats Grover Cleveland and Woodrow Wilson. Because there often were so few, if any, Democratic judges-in-waiting on the district courts within a particular circuit, when a vacancy arose or a position was created on these courts they usually went outside the district bench to find nominees, thereby sacrificing additional appointment opportunities.[47] Indeed, only one in every four (26 percent) of their appointees to the courts of appeals was elevated. Republicans obviously did not have this problem; elevations figured in more than half (56 percent) of their appellate court appointments. Sixty-eight appointments came from this one source alone compared to only 11 for Democrats.

Dynamics of Judicial Selection in the First Era

Republicans made 80 percent of all appointments to the lower bench during the 1869–1932 era. Breaking the total down by source, one out of every three appointments was to a new position, one of four (27 percent) represented voluntary turnover replacements, with the remainder coming from elevations (15 percent) and involuntary departures (25 percent). The Democratic tally underscores the party's subordinate status: only 18 percent of Cleveland and Wilson's appointments came from new seats—fully 15 percentage points lower than the Republican figure—whereas 42 percent came from involuntary departures, a number that is 17 percentage points higher. Republican administrations, then, took full advantage of the new methods of staffing the courts that were created for them by their colleagues in Congress. Roughly one-third (31 percent) of the Democrats' appointments came from replacing voluntary leavers, a figure that is actually higher than the Republican average (27 percent).[48] Further, Democratic jurists typically served longer terms than their GOP counterparts (15.4 versus 13.9 years), perhaps in an attempt to extend their stay on the bench to increase prospects of leaving during a same-party administration. The political dynamic to voluntary departures, in any case, favored Republicans. Seventy percent of all who left during their administrations were party affiliates. The partisan turnover rate during Democratic presidencies, by contrast, was 30 percentage points lower.[49]

Ironically the chief staffing source for Democrats came from cross-party appointments; that is, the commissioning of Democratic jurists by Republican presidents, whose 9 percent average in this regard yielded 36 appointees,[50] about one-third of the appointment totals of Cleveland and Wilson (see table 3.2). The shifting partisan balance in the Senate, the confirming chamber, informs when and why many of these appointments occurred. Two Republican administrations were significantly above, and two were below the norm. Those with relatively high cross-party appointment rates (Taft and Hoover) confronted Senates that averaged 42 percent Democratic, whereas those with low rates (Grant and Harding) dispatched nominees to the Senate where less than a third (31 percent) were so affiliated. Most cross-party appointments, then, were made when the Senate was more or less evenly balanced. Excluding appointments to the District of Columbia, which is of course without representation in the Senate, in nearly three out of every four cases (71 percent) the nominee's home state was represented by at least one senator from the opposition.[51] Indeed, 44 percent of the time the appointments were made to southern states, where both senators were usually Democrats, yet all but a handful of these (six) came during periods of near partisan parity in the Senate.

The politics of judgeship legislation customarily dictate that at least a judgeship or two go to the other party. After all, presidents must contend with the opposition on a wide range of policy matters, so a little slice of patronage here and there can reap larger dividends down the road. The Grant and Harding years aside—during which time all new positions went to Republicans—the data from 1869–1932 by and large support the proposition: 42 percent of all cross-party appointments were to new positions. Republicans nevertheless lost little in making these appointments, as half of the cross-party contingent placed on the courts of appeals were elevated and then replaced by members of the president's party on the district courts.

Judicial Appointments: The Presidential Record

Unified government, in sum, invariably biased judicial expansion from 1869 to 1932. Republicans controlled the first and second branches of government in 17 congresses, compared to but 4 for the Democrats, and so dictated the number and timing of additional judgeships. Most of the positions were filled by Republicans, of course, and most (81 percent) were postings to the district courts. The new district court positions, in turn, created a sizable pool of Republicans available for elevation. Indeed, Republicans were twice as likely to use the technique as a means of securing additional appointments to the federal bench. Finally, because there were so many more Republican judges in service, the potential of timing one's departure from the bench during a same-party presidency again favored the party of Lincoln. Yet the political balance in the Senate limited the universal appointment of Republicans. One-third of all Democrats receiving federal judgeships from 1869 to 1932 were commissioned by Republican presidents, mostly during periods of near partisan parity in the chamber. Republican judges unwittingly helped in another way. One out of every four of Grover Cleveland and Woodrow Wilson's appointments came from replacing Republicans who voluntarily left the bench during their tenure; all but one were replaced by same-party members.

The relative breakdown of Senate seats was a factor in cross-party appointments by Republicans, but not Democrats. Cleveland appointed only Democrats to federal judgeships, regardless of the partisan constellation in the Congress or the source of the opportunity.[52] Wilson's same-party appointment rate was second only to Cleveland's during the era. Democrats played their partisan hands to the fullest.

The figures in table 3.2 detail the source and number of appointments of all 16 administrations from 1869 to 1932, indicating the percentage of time the president's party controlled both houses of Congress. Table 3.3 details partisan percentages and changes and the size of presidential cohorts. The data illustrate the link between unified government, institutional growth, elevations, and recomposition of the bench: those receiving relatively few new positions (Hayes, Garfield/Arthur, Cleveland, and Wilson) frequently faced a Congress governed by the opposition, whereas the opposite was true for those usually enjoying partisan comity (Grant, Harrison, Roosevelt, Taft, Harding, Coolidge, and Hoover). The latter group additionally had a greater opportunity to elevate, a consequence of the swelling cadre of partisans on the district bench. These twin conditions, in turn, facilitated wholesale transformation of the federal courts.

The importance of unified government to placing a partisan majority on the bench nevertheless peaked by the turn of the century owing to the greater number of judges in service and thus the increased importance of turnover in the politics of appointment. Presidents Grant through McKinley, for example, averaged about 30 appointments in all, half the total of the Roosevelt through Hoover administrations. The ever-growing number of judicial offices meant that henceforth every administration could expect to carve out a political majority on the courts, unified government notwithstanding.[53] Woodrow Wilson is the notable example. First and foremost, 73 judges were commissioned by the 28th president, the second highest number in the era, and one sufficient to wrest control of the bench from the Republicans. Resignations and retirements accounted for 26 appointments, tying a record. Factoring in involuntary turnover, 78 percent ($N = 57$) of Wilson's appointments came from turnover alone. Indeed at the expiration of his administration, Wilson appointees occupied 53 percent of the lower federal bench, a percentage exceeded only by Grant and Roosevelt. His 98.6 percent partisan appointment rate niched a Democratic majority on the lower federal courts for the first time in 60 years.[54] This was a remarkable feat for a president whose party had been out of power for 16 years, who inherited the second most politically imbalanced bench since 1869, who was occupied by a global war for most of his presidency, and who wrestled with a politically divided Congress during the final two years of his presidency.[55]

Conclusion

An investigation of judicial appointments from 1869 to 1932 shows that during the nineteenth century control of the executive and legislative branches of government by the same party was instrumental to securing a political majority on the bench, because unified government determined the rate of bench expansion and, by extension, the frequency of replacement opportunities. Yet for twentieth century presidents the goal was reachable with or without partisan comity with Congress precisely because the size of the bench had grown so. The marked increase in judicial offices meant that an ever larger and in time predominant number of appointments would come from turnover, thereby virtually guaranteeing the president a majority on the courts. Unified government made the task easier, of course, but no longer was it necessary. Indeed, Woodrow Wilson was able to dissolve a 34-point Republican advantage in only eight years, primarily by filling vacancies. Presidents henceforth could realize such partisan control without the benefit of sizable numbers of additional positions, given adequate rates of turnover. In the next chapter we see how Dwight Eisenhower's approach to regaining partisan control of the bench in the absence of unified government and thus a limited number of new positions followed the course charted by Wilson.

CHAPTER 4

The Democrats Assume Power

> What has happened in this country that has created the necessity for these additional judges, almost all of them at the same time. . . . It is high time for this Congress to begin to set the example of economy in government, and here is a good chance to do it. It is time for us to quit playing pork-barrel politics.
>
> —Rep. Edward Rees (R–KS)

> I would not defend them [members of the Judicial Conference] against it [logrolling] either. When these judges get together and one says, "I want another judge in my district," and another judge says, "I want one in my district," you may imagine what happens, even though they wear the ermine.
>
> —Rep. Earl Michener (R–IL)

The election of Franklin Roosevelt in 1932 was a political watershed. The event marked only the fourth time since Reconstruction that a Democrat occupied the Oval Office, and the sixth time that the party controlled both the legislative and executive branches.[1] Democrats would be victorious in six out of the next eight presidential contests, holding a majority of seats in 15 of the ensuing 17 congresses. Indeed, during this span and through the election of Bill Clinton, Democratic presidents with only one exception worked with a Congress controlled by their party, whereas the opposite was true of Republicans, who labored under divided government for 13 out of 14 congresses.[2]

Roosevelt's election, in short, reversed a 72-year period of Republican hegemony, inaugurating an era of Democratic control of government. Roosevelt also was the only president in the post–Civil War era whose party increased its majority in both houses of Congress over the course of his first term and into the second, a feat not accomplished since the administrations of Thomas Jefferson and James Monroe.[3]

The 32d president came into office, then, with considerable assets as chief executive and party leader. He nevertheless inherited a federal bench in which nearly four out of every five judges on the lower courts, and six out of the nine on the High Court, were Republicans. The federal courts, of course, became the battleground between New Deal initiatives empowering government to intervene in the market and workplace to grapple with the Depression, and the Supreme Court's support for and sanction of the doctrine of laissez-faire.[4] As the scope of the economic malaise widened during Roosevelt's first term, and with each rejection by the courts of legislation to combat it, the question of the composition of the judiciary became not merely prominent, but the issue of the day. The ultimate victory went to FDR, for by the conclusion of his second term he achieved partisan control of the federal courts[5] and government regulation of the economy was here to stay.[6] The Court did gain some consolation, however, from the enactment of an enhanced retirement package.[7]

Understanding from previous chapters the part played by all three branches of government in shaping the institutional and partisan contours of the third, here as before the dynamics of appointments and departures are scrutinized during the 1933–68 period of Democratic political control. We highlight the singular role played by the Judicial Conference of the United States in bench expansion, exploring the association among caseload, Conference recommendations for additional judgeships, and the response of Congress under the alternative conditions of unified and divided government. The path of judgeship legislation is then traced from its introduction in Congress to its enactment, defeat, or delay, dissecting the connection between locale of the proposed judgeships, partisanship, and vote. Finally, we compare the size of both political and presidential judicial cohorts from the Roosevelt through the Johnson administrations and the ways in which each was attained.

Institutional Growth in the Middle Period

Given the increased importance of government in regulating the economy and in managing the nation's affairs more generally that began during the New Deal era, it is understandable that the executive and legislative branches would experience dramatic structural and personnel changes from 1933 to 1968. The Executive Office of the President, for example, whose staff numbered under 400 prior to the outbreak of the Second World War, swelled to nearly 2,000[8] by the conclusion of Lyndon Johnson's presidency. Two new cabinet departments were created during the interlude along with numerous White House and independent offices. Indeed, the number of regulatory offices alone doubled in a two-year period from 1933 to 1935.[9] Excepting the addition of four new senators and two representatives with the admission of Alaska and Hawaii to the Union in 1959, the size of the Congress remained constant during the era. Congressional staff was another matter. Numbering approximately 1,500 at the start of Roosevelt's presidency, it swelled to over 7,000 by 1968.[10] Paralleling the administrative changes in the second branch, new committees and especially subcommittees proliferated on Capitol Hill.

The number of judicial districts and circuits likewise changed little from 1933 to 1968. Federal courts and judges were another matter.[11] There were 181 permanent federal judgeships in 1933, 136 on the district courts and 45 on the courts of appeals.[12] The total more than doubled (to 432) by the conclusion of the Johnson administration. Politics played a large role in determining when and where new judicial offices were authorized in this era of Democratic Party control. The size of the bench grew about 4 percent annually from 1868 to 1932, compared to a 2.4 percent annual increase in the size of the bench during the previous 68 years. This yearly rate continued during the 1933 to 1968 era (see fig. 4.1). Administrative changes within the third branch facilitated the steady, step-level increases. The creation of the Judicial Conference of the United States in 1922, as we saw, transferred the initiative for recommending new judgeships from Congress to senior members of the federal judiciary. This body, in turn, routinely presented to Congress omnibus requests for new judicial offices. The recommendations were based on caseload statistics compiled, effective in 1939, by the auxiliary administrative organ of the federal courts, the Administrative Office of the United States Courts.

This approach that bundled requests lessened but did not eliminate the political haggling often accompanying and bedeviling bills of the past. The new method did serve, however, to accelerate the growth of the third branch by increasing over time both the number and especially the distribution of

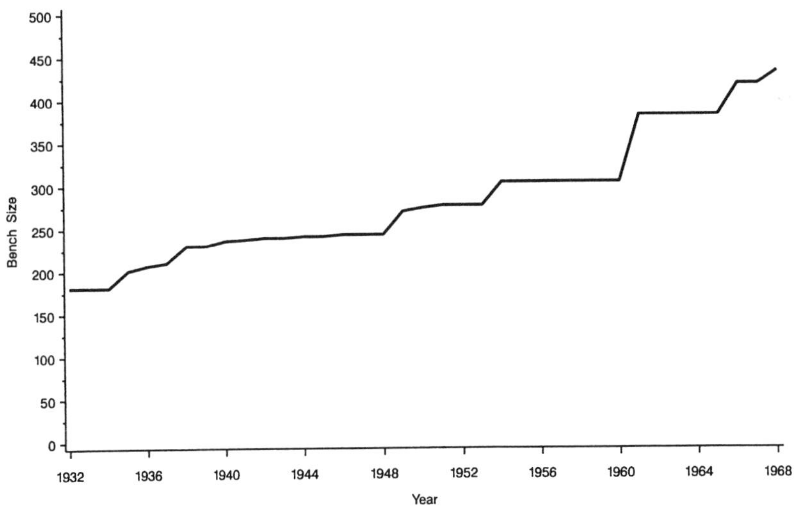

Fig. 4.1. Growth of the federal bench, 1933–68

judgeships. Consequently members of Congress from both parties received additional positions in their districts or states, which, in turn, limited dissent. Yet, as we show, the political-economic context affected both the timing and the outcome of omnibus judgeship legislation.

Roosevelt Administration

Beginning in the fall of 1930, the Judicial Conference in its *Annual Report* called for removal of restrictions on naming successors to judges appointed under the landmark omnibus judgeship act of September 14, 1922, and variously during 1925, 1928, and 1929. Congress created 25 positions in the 1922 bill (only two permanent[13]), primarily to deal with the onslaught of litigation stemming from the Volstead Act, yet wanted to retain control over them until "we shall have determined by actual experience whether these judgeships will be required as a permanent proposition."[14] Eight years later the Conference thought the time had come to convert the temporary lines, now totaling 17, into permanent ones, and add 5 new positions. The following year the recommendation was renewed, only this time with a request for 9 more judgeships. The 1932 report echoed that of the previous year: a call for 26 permanent judgeships, coming largely from conversions.

Normally, when the Oval Office and Capitol Hill are controlled by the same party, in this case by the Republicans, we would expect Congress to meet or to exceed the recommendations for additional judgeships.[15] The Depression changed the equation. Following the congressional elections of 1930, the Republican Party's commanding majority in the 71st Congress dwindled to a lone vote in the Senate, and was erased altogether in the House, where Democrats organized the chamber due to vacancies on the Republican side of the aisle.[16] The incumbent party was saddled with blame by voters for the dismal state of the economy, resulting in midterm election losses of 8 seats in the Senate and 51 in the House. The prospect for passage of an omnibus judgeship bill was nil under the circumstances. Moreover, the Hoover administration's own Budget Bureau rejected the request on grounds that the government could not afford to finance the positions.[17] The 31st president, at any rate, garnered only five new judgeships in his last two years in office.[18] Subsequently in September 1934 the Judicial Conference pared the number of recommended positions to 16, all but 4 of which would simply convert temporary to permanent.[19]

On January 24, 1935, Representative Arthur D. Healey (D–MA) introduced H.R. 4665, a resolution calling for the conversion of a temporary Massachusetts district judgeship. The death of Judge Lowell, who had held the temporary position, left the single-district state with only two judges.[20] Although later in the session Congress would consider the Judicial Conference recommendation to convert all such temporary lines, Healey asked that disposition of Lowell's position be extracted from the omnibus bill and given expeditious treatment due to extraordinary caseload problems in the Massachusetts district court. The House dispatched the bill by voice vote on May 20.[21]

Healey's bill cleared the Senate without significant controversy, yet S. 481 contained amendments that converted 14 other temporary positions. The politicking that accompanied Senate approval of its bill rankled several members of the House, especially John J. O'Connor (D–NY), who complained that, "The question before the House at the present time is whether this body can legislate or whether it must swallow everything which another body does."[22] O'Connor and his allies argued that if indeed the temporary positions were to be converted, then justification should be made on a case-by-case basis rather than in omnibus fashion. House backers of the Senate version responded that the bill was almost identical to one under consideration by the House Judiciary Committee. Also, of the 15 positions in the Senate bill, 12 were in districts targeted by the Judicial Conference and two others were endorsed by the attorney general.[23]

The House debate and vote (189–125) on the measure divided evenly along party lines. Ten of the eleven representatives speaking in favor were Democrats.[24] Three of the five voicing opposition were Republicans, with the two Democrats (O'Connor, and William D. McFarlane of Texas) being outside their party's mainstream on this issue.[25] Seventy percent of the Democrats who voted endorsed the resolution, whereas 69 percent of the Republicans did not. Twenty-two Republicans joined 163 Democrats to carry the bill.[26] Breaking down the tally further, among supporters, those whose states were to receive judgeships ($N = 98$) were only slightly more likely to vote for the bill than those whose states were not ($N = 91$). However, 17 of the 22 Republicans voting "yea" came from states slated to receive new judgeships whereas a majority of the Democrats supporting the legislation ($N = 85$) did not. Voting, then, was mostly a function of party affiliation, although the location of the judgeships improved the chances of Republican support.[27]

What was to become the Act of May 31, 1938 (PL 75-555) was distinctive perhaps more for its genesis than for the number of new positions authorized (20).[28] The Judicial Conference in its 1937 *Annual Report* recommended 4 additional appellate and 12 district judgeships.[29] The House and Senate in the preceding Congress passed a bill to reorganize the judiciary, yet—while proclaiming their willingness to create sufficient new judgeships to dispatch judicial business—deferred the question until it could be given further study. During the first session of the 75th Congress (1937), ad hoc committees of both the House and Senate Judiciary Committees were impaneled for that purpose.[30] The committees reviewed caseload data and the requests of legislators and sitting judges, and conducted a spate of interviews, all of which produced bipartisan agreement that they had done a thorough job (although somewhat less consensus was achieved on the recommendations).[31]

Following a review of the reports of the Conference, the attorney general, and its own investigation of staffing needs, the Senate Judiciary reported S. 3691, a bill providing 5 appellate and 14 new district court positions.[32] Debate lasted only one day. Outside of a few statements regarding the mushrooming of the federal judiciary,[33] most of the remarks involved justification of recommended positions by home-state senators.[34] The measure, at any rate, enjoyed widespread support from both sides of the aisles. The Senate approved S. 3691 by a vote of 71–7 on March 30. Only one of the seven dissenters (Copeland of New York) represented a state slated to receive a new position. Ninety-five percent ($N = 61$) of the Democrats who voted backed the measure, compared to 70 percent ($N = 7$) of the Republicans.[35] Three of the seven GOP supporters came from states in line to receive new judgeships.

House consideration of the bill was considerably more turgid. Members who spoke in favor of the bill, like their Senate colleagues, generally were from states targeted for new positions. Opponents took one of two tacks. One was to decry the senseless growth of an already bloated judiciary.[36] Another, reminiscent of the debate over the 1935 bill, was to continue resisting the very notion of omnibus legislation, arguing instead that positions should be justified and voted upon on a case-by-case basis, thereby separating the wheat from the chaff in bench expansion.[37] Ultimately the substitute version of S. 3691 passed the House on May 3, 1938 without a recorded roll call, by a vote of 117 to 37, and the conference committee report was approved by both houses of Congress two weeks later.[38] The bill provided for 5 appellate and 15 district judgeships (3 temporary[39]), and was signed into law on May 31, 1938.

Consideration of the 1940 judgeship bill was infused with the partisan politics of a presidential election year that were inflamed by Roosevelt's unprecedented run for a third consecutive term in office. Several Republicans were unabashed in efforts to delay any enlargement of the judiciary until after the election, when a Republican might sit in the Oval Office.[40] Members of the minority party in both the House and Senate went so far as to oppose new positions even in their own states.[41] Indeed, lobbying campaigns were orchestrated in which members of state bar associations and even judges on the courts in line to receive the positions would write or wire that judicial business was being transacted expeditiously with the existing complement of judges. In the Senate, separate amendments were offered to eliminate each position in the bill. The Democrats, for their part, trotted out statistic after statistic to justify the new offices.

The Judicial Conference recommended additional positions for the Sixth and Eighth Circuits, and eight district judgeships. Upon review of those recommendations the House Judiciary Committee reported a bill containing seven positions, all of which were endorsed by the Conference and the attorney general. Amendments would add a second seat on the Eighth Circuit and positions in the Northern District of Illinois and the Western District of Oklahoma. The Republicans were especially irate over the Illinois seat, which was not requested by the Judicial Conference.[42] As passed by the House on March 14, 1940 by a 210–137 roll call vote, H.R. 7079 provided for three appellate and seven new district judgeships.[43] Similar to the vote in 1935, support divided along party lines. Ninety-four percent (N = 193) of the Democrats voting on the resolution supported it whereas 89 percent of the Republicans (N = 122) did not. The overwhelming majority of those in favor (N = 153) represented states that would not get additional judges from the bill. All but eight were Democrats. Eight of the 15 Republicans endorsing the bill, by contrast, were from states in line for additional judges.

The Senate bill originally provided for eight new seats, and the Judiciary Committee offered an amendment for the additional Eighth Circuit position, which succeeded. Following two days of lugubrious and often acrimonious debate, the Senate approved the bill by voice vote on April 15.[44] The substitute version of H.R. 7079 authorized nine new positions. Going into conference, there were some significant discrepancies in the two versions of the bills.[45] The conference committee reported back a bill in which positions endorsed in either the House or Senate drafts were included, for a total of twelve. What was to become Public Law 76-521 was approved without fanfare by both houses of Congress and signed by President Roosevelt on May 24, 1940.[46]

No additional omnibus acts were legislated during the remainder of Roosevelt's presidency. Indeed only eight permanent positions were created between 1941 and 1945, all but two coming from conversions as the exigencies of waging World War II consumed the time and energy of the White House.[47] The defeat and surrender of German and Japanese forces in April and August of 1945 and their military occupation and reorganization the following year occupied the attention of the new Truman administration. Meanwhile, the 1946 congressional elections returned the Republicans to power in both the Senate and the House for the first time in twenty years. Midway through his first term in office, Harry Truman confronted a Congress controlled by the Republicans.

Truman Administration

Whereas Roosevelt always worked with substantial Democratic majorities in Congress, the 33d president faced a Congress where Republicans in 1947 and 1948 held healthy majorities of 58 votes in the House and 6 in the Senate. The relationship between the two branches was heated, and the effect of this brief and bitter interlude of divided government on new positions was predictable: the 80th Congress authorized no new judgeships.[48] Meanwhile in its September 1948 *Annual Report,* the Judicial Conference called for 23 new positions, all but 3 permanent.

Truman's election in 1948 and the Democrats' recapture of Congress all but guaranteed enactment of an omnibus bill. What is distinctive about the legislative history of H.R. 4963/S. 52 is the virtually unanimous agreement—on "both sides of the aisle"—on the need for more judges to unclog the federal courts. Indeed, even the two most vocal House critics of the Roosevelt bills spoke in support of the 1949 legislation, the first in more than nine years.[49]

The Judicial Conference in its March 1949 *Annual Report* recommended 6 new appellate and 23 district judgeships.[50] The bill reported by the House Committee on the Judiciary provided for four fewer positions. The House bill was more tentative in that it reduced the number of new seats in two districts from two to one and balked at converting two temporary positions. Most of the floor debate was on an amendment introduced by Kenneth B. Keating (R–NY) mandating that no more than two-thirds of the positions authorized by the act be filled by members of the same political party. The amendment generated a protracted debate on Article III of the Constitution, the intentions of the Framers, the separation of powers doctrine, the idea of an independent and nonpartisan judiciary, and the political reality of whether a bill with this restriction could elude a presidential veto. Obviously a fallback position for the minority who could not deny the need for an omnibus bill, the amendment was defeated and the unamended measure was approved by voice vote on June 16.[51] The Senate Judiciary Committee bill authorized 27 new seats. Two floor amendments to convert temporary positions to permanent (one of which was recommended by the Judicial Conference) were approved, bringing the figure to 29.[52] The bill, with amendments, passed by voice vote on June 27, 1949.

The House and Senate versions that were sent to conference differed in two significant ways—the Senate bill authorized four more positions, and there were substantial differences in the restrictions placed on several others. The leitmotiv of the eventual product was that the House receded on the number of positions and the Senate deferred to the House on the restrictions (including elimination of a Senate amendment regarding D.C. district positions). Although the number of new seats ultimately legislated by Congress was identical to the total recommended by the Judicial Conference (29),[53] Congress was somewhat more generous by authorizing permanent seats in two instances where the Conference recommendation was for temporary offices.[54] Both chambers approved the conference report without controversy or debate. On August 3, 1949, President Truman signed into law the largest expansion of the federal bench in history.[55]

One year later the nation was again gripped in conflict abroad. The Korean War dragged on until June 1953, ultimately damaging the public standing and particularly the political clout of the Truman administration. The midterm elections reflected the growing dissatisfaction of the electorate with Truman's party, who saw their advantage in the House shrink to 35 seats and in the Senate to only 1. It is not surprising, then, that a resolution introduced in the 82d Congress to expand the federal bench (S. 1203) failed in the House as Republicans—anticipating victory in the upcoming elections—united to turn back the bill. A few months later the reins of government indeed were in their hands.

Eisenhower Administration

It did not take long for the 83d Congress to resurrect and enact the omnibus judgeship legislation that stalled in the previous session. S. 15 broke the short-lived record of the 1949 act: the bill provided for 43 new positions.[56] The Judicial Conference had requested 37 new judgeships.[57] The huge increase recommended by the Conference was not de novo to that Congress,[58] but rather was an accumulated list owing to the refusal of Capitol Hill to act on any recommendations for five years. A Conference-sanctioned expansion had languished in the House during the previous Congress, for instance, occasioned by what several Democrats charged was a rear guard delay by Republicans who hoped to capture the presidency in the 1952 elections.[59] The Senate Judiciary Committee bill provided for 42 new positions, five more than called for by the Judicial Conference. Although a handful of senators rose to justify the new judgeships in their states, there was only one amendment offered to alter the committee recommendations with regard to new seats[60] and the bill cleared the Senate by voice vote.

The House Committee on the Judiciary was more temperate: its version provided for 30 new positions (3 appellate and 27 district).[61] Throughout the floor debate the sentiment was repeatedly expressed that with the cost of each new position being in the neighborhood of $50,000 annually (including support personnel and overhead), the Senate proposal simply had to be pared back. Understandably this led representatives who had positions in the Senate bill deleted in the House version to bemoan how the speed and therefore the quality of justice in their states would be compromised ("justice delayed is justice denied"). Departing from the usual justifications based on caseload statistics, legislators resorted to arguments that their states needed judges more than others, and in the extreme that one district in a state needed relief more than another district in that same state.[62]

The House version ultimately provided for 30 new positions, a figure identical to the recommendations of that chamber's Judiciary Committee. The bills went to conference, but the managers were unable to agree on compromise language before the close of the First Session of the 83d Congress. The conference resumed its negotiations early in 1954, and by the end of January was able to report a bill providing for 34 new positions (3 circuit, 31 district). The conference report walked a delicate line between the House and Senate versions: the Senate receded to fewer positions in districts in which it had sanctioned multiple slots, the House consented to positions in states it had not initially targeted.

The Senate approved the bill without fanfare, but the minority in the House took issue with certain features it considered blatantly partisan. What irked the Democrats most—especially Emanuel Celler (D–NY), erstwhile chair of the Judiciary Committee—was the provision for new district judgeships in Utah and Nevada, which were not included in the recommendations of the Judicial Conference and hardly seemed justified on the basis of caseload statistics.[63] The final bill—passed without a recorded vote in either house—included 5 district court positions that were not recommended by the Judicial Conference. Nine of the 10 senators from those states were Republicans; the exception was Patrick A. McCarran from Nevada, who while chair of the Judiciary Committee in previous congresses extended all kinds of collegial gestures to Republicans. Public Law 83-294 was signed by President Eisenhower on February 10, 1954.

The Democrats regained control of the Congress following the 1954 elections. The party's hold on the Congress grew steadily from a 29-vote margin in the House and a bare majority in the Senate in 1955 to advantages of 130 seats in the House and 30 in the Senate in 1960. Bills submitted to augment the size of the bench not surprisingly were stalled or tabled in the Senate Judiciary Committee during the final six years of Eisenhower's presidency. Indeed, only four positions were authorized during this span, three coming from the granting of statehood to Alaska and Hawaii.[64]

While the Democrats stymied Eisenhower's domestic legislative agenda[65] in general and his request for additional judgeships in particular, the Judicial Conference's recommended judgeship list ballooned from 14 positions in September 1954 to 71 by March 1961. The director of the Administrative Office of the United States Courts, Henry P. Chandler, entered the fray.[66] Chandler, the only director the Office had ever known, raised the ire of Senate Majority Leader Lyndon Johnson with a series of reprimands of the Congress for its failure to alleviate the "caseload crunch" on the courts by authorizing additional judgeships. The missive from 1956 was typical:

> The congestion and delay in civil cases in the federal courts is a serious evil and unfortunate . . . it is increasing. There is no one remedy. More judges are not the entire answer, but they are part of it, and a necessary part.[67]

Incredibly, in the very next report Chandler wrote

> The general trend in the volume of cases begun in the courts [of appeals] has been upward since 1947 which probably is the result of an increase of 49 district judgeships since that year and a very substantial increase in the number of trials in the district courts.[68]

Thus we find supply creating its own demand.

Not to be outflanked, Johnson challenged the caseload procedures used by the Judicial Conference in a stinging letter demanding additional and more refined supporting evidence for recommended positions, and contending that judges should process cases more efficiently in any event. He further asked that Chandler

> . . . provide me with a detailed description of what each Federal judicial district has done to improve the management efficiency of its courts in order to expedite the handling of its cases. . . . I do not believe it is possible to evaluate the need for a particular new judge without the above information.[69]

In the course of the exchange Chandler retired and was replaced by the more conciliatory Warren Olney III.[70] The new director demurred that his office could not comply with the demand for data for particular courts because

> Such information can only be secured by field surveys of the administration of each court—surveys which the Administrative Office is not presently equipped to make. . . . The attitude of the Congress with respect to increasing the number of Federal judgeships . . . shows the need for improvement in judicial administration.[71]

Johnson's attack of the Conference's statistical procedures was all but forgotten two years later as the incoming Kennedy administration poised in anticipation of receiving the largest number of additional judgeships ever, an increase more than double the record allotment given to Eisenhower.

Kennedy Administration

Citing the need "to relieve serious congestion and delays in many Federal Courts,"[72] on February 9, 1961, President Kennedy asked Congress to create

9 new appellate and 50 district court judgeships based upon the recommendations of the Judicial Conference.[73] There had been no omnibus bill since the 34 positions legislated in 1954. Despite the grousing of Senator Richard B. Russell (D–GA) that "The net effect of this will be to increase the malignant influence and tyrannical power of the present Supreme Court,"[74] the fate of S. 912 never really was in doubt. After all, Democrats retained a firm grip on Congress, Republicans had controlled the Oval Office for the preceding eight years, and Kennedy's election locked in the condition of partisan unity.

Republicans needled and occasionally railed against their counterparts for this exercise in judicial pork barrel politics, especially since the latter had steadfastly refused to grant the Eisenhower administration's wish for 35 new positions in 1960. Wondering aloud why there was such a pressing need for new judges in 1961 but not in 1960, Senator Kenneth B. Keating (R–NY) stated: "The present urgency for action . . . smacks strongly of patronage politics."[75]

Throughout the process the question was not whether there would be a bill, but rather how many additional judgeships it would contain. By congressional standards the measure actually sailed through, being signed by the president (PL 87-36) only five months (July 11, 1961) after it was introduced. The Senate passed a slightly amended version by voice vote on March 3 calling for 10 appellate and 60 district court judgeships.[76] The House followed suit on April 19 on a 336–76 roll call vote that broke with tradition in that a majority of Republicans supported the measure. An overwhelming number of the voting members of both parties were from states slated to receive new positions.[77] All told, 250 Democrats and 86 Republicans favored the resolution. All 76 of those opposed were Republicans. Of the 336 supporters of the bill, 283 were from states targeted for additional judgeships. Of these, 208 were Democrats and 75 were Republicans. Thus, 87 percent of the GOP supporters and 83 percent of the Democrats represented states on the receiving end for new positions. After 40 years of wrangling over the matter, Congress found a tried and tested way to elicit bipartisan support for judgeship legislation—spread the pork around—and at least in this area they have been doing so ever since. There were minor differences between the two versions (in the number and location of judges), but the customary logrolling resulted in a successful conference version that created 10 appellate and 63 district court positions.[78]

In the aftermath of Kennedy's assassination, public sympathy translated into a landslide victory for the Democrats in the 1964 general election that roughly paralleled the triumph of 1932.[79] Meanwhile in September 1964 the Judicial Conference moved to a quadrennial format for its survey of judgeship needs, staggering the timing of its overview of the district and circuit courts. The new procedure resulted in the Johnson administration receiving two omnibus bills, one exclusively designated for the courts of appeals (PL 90-347).[80]

Johnson Administration

The importance of unity between the president and Congress is again illustrated by the facile enactment of S. 1666, a bill ultimately authorizing 10 new appellate and 35 district court judgeships, making it second only to the Kennedy bill in the number of additional positions (see fig. 4.1). Slightly altering its March 1965 list of proposed judgeships, in September the Judicial Conference recommended 43 new positions (9 appellate, 34 district), once again citing overcrowded dockets and heavy caseload. The Senate endorsed the legislation by voice vote on June 30.[81] With little dissent (371–23; the dissenters were 18 Republicans and 5 southern Democrats), the House passed and returned to the Senate an amended bill adding another seat in the new Central District of California on March 2, 1966. Perhaps the clearest indication of support for the bill was that the Senate accepted the House amendments by a voice vote on March 8, thereby obviating the impaneling of a conference committee.[82] Only one position requested by the Conference was not legislated, whereas the Congress authorized three that were not on the list submitted by the Conference.[83] Bipartisan support for the measure once again was expressed, along with a generous dose of self-interest. Eighty-seven percent (N = 116) of the Republicans who voted, and 98 percent of the Democrats (N = 255), supported the legislation. Of the supporters, 221 (60 percent) represented states targeted for new judgeships, 141 Democrats and 80 Republicans. Sixty-nine percent of the Republican supporters came from states slated to receive additional judges, compared to 55 percent for the Democrats.

The administration received a second omnibus bill in 1968 that can be viewed as a complement to its predecessor, in that it affected positions only on the courts of appeals, four of which were created as temporary lines by PL 89-373. The Judicial Conference list submitted to Congress called for 12 positions.[84] All 12 were authorized by PL 90-347, along with an additional judgeship.[85] Here it was apparent that relief in the form of more judges was needed. Caseload on these courts had nearly doubled from the level of 1954, reaching 107 cases per judge by 1968, a record for the 1933–68 era.

It is evident from the legislative history of judgeship acts during the New Deal through Great Society years that their fate rested on whether the president's party held a majority in the Congress. All eight omnibus measures were passed during periods of unified government. Legislation introduced in times of divided control uniformly failed, a pattern documented during the 1869–1932 years of Republican hegemony as well. Indeed, all but 4 of the 251

TABLE 4.1. Bench Expansion during Periods of Unified and Divided Government, 1933–68 (new permanent positions)

Circuit Courts		
	Congress	
Administration	Unified	Divided
Republican	3	0
Democratic	49	0
Total	52	0

District Courts		
	Congress	
Administration	Unified	Divided
Republican	25	4
Democratic	170	0
Total	195	4

judgeships authorized by various and sundry acts of Congress from 1933 to 1968 came during years when the president's party governed Congress (see table 4.1), a condition that obtained 78 percent of the time.

Political considerations served to inflate considerably the number of authorized positions. We find little evidence that partisanship affected the Judicial Conference's list of proposed judgeships. Time and time again, however, Congress exceeded the number requested, authorizing additional judgeships well beyond what caseload figures would support. Take the example of three district courts with heavy caseloads, the Southern Districts of New York, Texas, and California (the Central District after 1966). Between 1934, a stable year to benchmark the start of the assessment period, and 1968, civil and criminal filings on these courts increased 62 percent in New York, 114 percent in Texas, and 125 percent in California. The number of additional positions, however, ballooned to 167 percent, 600 percent, and 157 percent, respectively. Further, caseload on the courts fluctuated markedly even while bench size rose constantly. Indeed, in the history of the lower federal courts, only a handful of permanent judicial offices have ever been taken away by Congress, none since the omnibus format took hold in 1935. Undoubtedly the procedures employed by the Judicial Conference and its agents to measure workload are less than perfect.[86] What matters is that the data are translated into estimates having an air of authenticity and authority that Congress ultimately accepts and, more often than not, augments. Moreover, by the 1960s, judgeship bills were nearly nationwide in scope,[87] so bipartisan support swelled, resulting in record-breaking institutional growth.

Appointment Politics in the Middle Period

The Democratic Party's dominance of the 1933–68 era is reflected in the distribution of judgeships by party of administration and majority party in Congress. Reversing the situation from 1869 to 1932, 88 percent of the permanent positions ($N = 219$) were created by Democratic Congresses for Democratic presidents, who occupied the White House nearly three out of every four years during the era. The breakdown by type of position, district or appellate, further underscores the grip Democrats had on the machinery of government. Eighty-five percent of the district judgeships ($N = 170$) went to Democratic administrations, as did all but 3 of the 52 (94.2 percent) positions on the courts of appeals (see table 4.1). Democrats, then, were far better situated to engineer partisan control of the judiciary: 242 new positions were filled during the Roosevelt through Johnson years; all but 34 (14 percent) were appointed by Democrats.

Seven hundred seventy-five judges were commissioned during the era, and only 47 were not members of the president's party. Breaking down cross-party appointments by level of court shows a slightly higher percentage (6.5 percent) on the courts of appeals than on the district courts (5.4 percent), percentages that conform to the historical pattern. Such appointments are more likely to be made to the appellate bench because the Oval Office and the Justice Department can, for nominees from the district courts, take into consideration judicial track record. Thus, by advancing members of the opposition to these courts, presidents are not really sacrificing all that much. Those so selected are likely to be ideologically acceptable to the administration, and their position on the district courts can be filled by a same-party member in any event.[88] Not having such decisional barometers to inform appointments to the district courts, party affiliation becomes more important and so proportionally fewer cross-party appointments are made.

Nevertheless when the type of appointment is factored in (to a new position or to fill a vacancy), we find that one out of every four cross-party appointments to the district courts ($N = 32$) went to fill a new position, yet none to the courts of appeals. There is a simple explanation for the discrepancy, deriving from the politics of omnibus judgeship legislation. In an era in which the number of additional positions was mushrooming from 15 (Act of August 19, 1935) to 76 (PL 87-36), presidents could well afford to appoint an occasional judge from the opposition either as a sop or a reward for supporting the measures. It would make sense, nevertheless, for the appointments to be made to the less prestigious district courts.[89]

Delving further into the politics of cross-party appointments to these courts, their frequency seems to covary with the number of opposition party senators in the state. Excluding the District Court of the District of Columbia, which of course is without representation in the U.S. Senate, in all other cases at least one senator was from the opposition; 58 percent of the time both were so affiliated. There is a modest association between divided government and cross-party appointments. All but two of Eisenhower's Democratic nominees were sent forward after the Republicans lost control of Congress. Conversely, Roosevelt had the lowest cross-party appointment rate and always worked with congresses where Democrats held solid majorities.[90]

Voluntary Turnover and Partisan Change

We detailed in earlier chapters the rise in importance of retirement, which became an option in 1869 and an especially attractive one with the advent of senior status in 1919. Between 1869 and 1932, replacements for those vacating by either retiring or resigning comprised about one out of every four appointments. Subsequent legislation greatly improved the retirement package, giving senior service retirees the same raises their full-time colleagues received (1948 act), establishing an early retirement with full-pay provision (1954 act), and setting up a survivor's annuities fund (1956 act). Responding to the improved emoluments, retirements rose steadily from 1933 to 1968: 35 percent of all appointments were to replace those who either retired or resigned (see table 4.2).[91]

Voluntary turnover is not only a fertile—and since 1933—*the* chief source of appointment opportunities; it often is politically timed. Fifty-seven percent of those voluntarily relinquishing their judgeships did so during an administration governed by their party. Meanwhile, average length of service also rose from 11.5 years in the preretirement era (1789–1868), to 13.3 in the Republican-controlled period wherein the initial benefits were enacted (1869–1932), to 16.4 during the Democrats' heyday. The increasing length of service is obviously tied to improved retirement benefits, yet it may have a political basis as well—judges extending their stay on the bench to increase the odds of

TABLE 4.2. Sources of Appointments to the Lower Federal Courts, 1933–68 (by positions filled)

Source	Percentage of Total
New seats	31.7%
Elevations	11.2
Voluntary turnover replacements	35.9
Involuntary turnover replacements	21.2
Total	775

departing during an administration under control of their party. If there is merit to this hypothesis, then we should find Republican jurists serving longer than Democrats during the Roosevelt and Truman years as they await a GOP administration. The opposite should be true of Democrats during the Kennedy and Johnson years, who served through Eisenhower's term to retire during these ensuing Democratic administrations. The data support the argument. The average length of service of Republicans increased from 16.4 years under Roosevelt to 21.1 during Truman's presidency, and peaked at 24.5 years under Eisenhower. Meanwhile the average tenure of Democrats, which ranged from 14 to 14.7 years during the Roosevelt and Truman years, climbed to 17.8 years during Eisenhower's presidency.[92]

We saw in chapter 3 that during the 1869–1932 era, Republican jurists were more prone to retire or to resign during a same-party presidency. There were, of course, many more Republican appointees and administrations then and so these judges had plenty of opportunity to harmonize their departures from the bench, thereby enabling their replacement by younger same-party members. The pattern flip-flopped from 1933 to 1968. There now were vastly larger numbers of Democrats being commissioned—particularly to newly authorized positions—and, of course, more Democratic administrations. We would expect, then, that voluntary turnover replacements would be an especially bountiful fount of appointments. Two hundred and three judges retired or resigned during Democratic administrations, 71 percent of the total. Sixty percent (N = 120) were affiliates of the party. The percentages steadily climbed, from 34 percent during Roosevelt's presidency, a time when, at least initially, there were very few Democrats in service (22.2 percent), to 52 percent for Truman. The trend continued after Eisenhower left office. The same-party leaving rate soared to 83 percent under Kennedy, and an equally impressive 75 percent during Johnson's presidency.

Voluntary turnover proved to be a boon to Eisenhower's appointment opportunities as well. Considering that his administration followed 20 years of uninterrupted Democratic occupation of the Oval Office, it is noteworthy that almost half (49 percent) of those who either retired or resigned during his tenure were Republicans. Remarkably, this GOP cohort[93] stayed in service an average of 28 years (12 years longer than the subperiod mean) so as to retire from the bench during the first available Republican administration in the post–New Deal era.

Elevations and Appointment Politics

Elevations from one court level to another are an intricate form of turnover, in that they also create vacancies and so afford presidents opportunities to make additional appointments. They are increasingly popular as well. Seventy-four were made from 1933 to 1968,[94] about the same number as for the preceding era (1869–1932), but in half the time. All told, two out of every five appointees to the courts of appeals were elevated during the subperiod. Fourteen percent were not affiliated with the party of the president, which is more than twice the norm. Even so, we have mentioned repeatedly that presidents usually give up little by elevating judges of the opposition party to these courts: an additional appointment is garnered, some bipartisan spirit can be displayed, and the nominee's decisions are probably in tune with the judicial orientation of the administration.[95]

We would expect that Democratic presidents in promoting judges to the appellate courts would be better positioned to take advantage of the vastly greater number of Democrats on the district courts. Indeed as this pool deepened so too did the yearly number of elevations. Averaging 1.4 during Roosevelt's presidency and 1.5 under Truman, the number grew to 2.7 during Kennedy's abbreviated presidency, and to 3.8 under Johnson.

Eisenhower again bucked the trend by elevating more judges (18) than his counterparts. This was done by seeding the ranks of the district courts with Republicans during the first term and then elevating mostly his own appointees to the appellate bench in the second: 25 percent were elevated from 1953–56, compared to 60 percent afterward.

Partisan and Institutional Change on the Courts

It is evident from the data in table 4.3 that the appointment mix varies for each administration. Roosevelt—who served longest and always enjoyed partisan comity with the Congress—commissioned the most judges (185), who were distributed almost equally in the three categories of new positions, voluntary turnover replacements, and involuntary turnover replacements. Eisenhower registered the second highest number of appointments (172), but working with a politically compatible Congress only 25 percent of the time explains why his percentage of appointments to new seats (19.2 percent) was well below that of the others. The 34th president relied instead on voluntary turnover replacements to staff the courts, using elevations whenever possible to compound appointment opportunities. Forty-four percent ($N = 72$) of Eisenhower's appointments came from turnover, the highest percentage of the five. Kennedy did exactly the opposite, making 57 percent of his appointments to new positions, and only 23 percent to replace voluntary leavers. Truman and Johnson's appointment tendencies more or less mirrored one another except where filling vacancies was concerned: involuntary turnover replacements provided a sizable proportion of Truman's appointments (28.1 percent) whereas voluntary departures (42.8 percent) did so for Johnson.

Finally, table 4.4 details the extent of partisan and institutional change on the lower federal courts. Franklin Roosevelt, who inherited the most politically

TABLE 4.3. Appointments to the Lower Federal Courts, 1933–68 (by positions filled)

Administration	Unified Government	New Positions	Elevations	Voluntary Turnover Replacements	Involuntary Turnover Replacements	Circuit Court	District Court	Total
F. Roosevelt	100%	30.8%	9.2%	30.3%	29.7%	52	133	185
Truman	75	25.8	9.4	36.7	28.1	27	101	128
Eisenhower	25	19.2	12.8	44.2	23.8	45	127	172
Kennedy	100	57.3	6.5	23.4	12.9	20	104	124
L. Johnson	100	31.3	11.4	42.8	14.5	41	125	166

TABLE 4.4. Partisan and Institutional Change on the Lower Federal Courts, 1933–68

Administration	Partisan Appointment Rate	Partisan Proportion on the Bench (swing)	Presidential Cohort
F. Roosevelt	95.7%	70.0% (+47.8)	64.8%
Truman	92.2	81.7 (+11.7)	45.3
Eisenhower	94.8	50.0 (+31.7)	50.2
Kennedy	91.1	60.2 (+10.2)	33.8
L. Johnson	94.6	70.5 (+10.3)	39.4

imbalanced bench, had the highest same-party appointment rate, engineered the largest partisan turnaround, and far and away posted the most extensive cohort. Eisenhower ranked second in all of these respects, which is impressive in that he served four years fewer and usually faced a Democratic Congress. Truman's lower partisan appointment percentage can be attributed to the constraints of appointment politics during the acrimonious stint of the 80th Congress. Truman appointees nonetheless made up nearly half of the bench by the conclusion of his term. Kennedy's same-party appointment rate also was below the norm but for a different reason: with a record number of new appointments to make, the 35th president could well afford to commission a number of Republicans. The extent of partisan change on the bench also was lower than average (10.2 percent), as was the size of the Kennedy cohort at the time of his assassination. Johnson's coterie was slightly higher than average (39.4 percent). All five presidents left office with political majorities on the courts, and in the case of the Democrats, substantial ones.

Conclusion

When Franklin Roosevelt assumed office Democrats occupied only about one out of every five seats (22 percent) on the lower federal bench. That figure pegged out at 70.5 percent by the conclusion of Lyndon Johnson's presidency. The party's domination of the federal courts from 1933 to 1968 was as complete as its counterpart's during its 1869–1932 hegemony, and as fleeting. Roosevelt reversed the GOP majority in less than two terms in office. It would take Johnson's predecessors, Nixon and Ford, even less time to return the favor. Subsequently, Presidents Carter and Reagan would orchestrate partisan majorities within the span of a single term.

Clearly since the turn of the century the party capturing the White House ultimately controls the federal bench as well, regardless of whether government is unified or not. Same-party control of the executive and legislative branches facilitates the process through bench expansion, which, in time, translates into an ever larger number of retirees. Their growing numbers, in turn, ensure that even presidents serving during times of divided government (e.g., Eisenhower) can place partisan majorities on the courts by filling vacancies. Political control of the judiciary, in short, comes and goes with victory or defeat in presidential elections.

The fount of appointments, in sum, depends upon the condition of government. Periods of unified control lead to major expansions in the number of judgeships, whereas under divided government turnover provides the core of appointment opportunities. Such departures are often politically timed, as turnover and length-of-service rates by party show. The judges, then, are active players in the partisan transformation of their institution. Indeed, voluntary leavers create the most important staffing source, replacements. Coming full circle, the ranks of this group are seeded by the proliferation of new positions.

We have documented the politics of bench expansion, showing that omnibus increases took place only when the president's party controlled Congress. Further, Congress typically created more positions than called for by the Judicial Conference, and the allotment was usually significantly greater than the concomitant rise in caseload, the basis for additional judgeships. The Conference and Congress, in any event, never seriously considered capping the size of the judiciary, much less eliminating offices during periods of stable or declining caseload. Instead the omnibus format, which was the subject of considerable debate and controversy during the 1920s and 1930s, became the staple for altering, that is augmenting the size of, the bench. Indeed the omnibus legislation of the Truman, Eisenhower, and Kennedy administrations set one record after another for the largest number of new positions, an explosion that was detonated on Capitol Hill. The judgeships were conveniently distributed across most of the states, producing bipartisan support. This spirit of cooperation carried over into the presidency of Nixon—who, parenthetically, became the first to receive an omnibus bill from an opposition Congress—and so growth continued unabated. Meanwhile, retirements were to reach record levels while length of service declined, producing a so-called crisis in judicial service during the 1970s.[96] An ever-expanding bench subject to marked turnover, massive alterations in personnel, and wide swings in partisanship, then, was a legacy of the New Deal through Great Society years.

CHAPTER 5

Appointment Politics in an Age of Divided Government

Far from being the tenuous and unmeaningful victory suggested by critical observers, the election of Richard M. Nixon as President of the United States in November, 1968, bespoke the end of the New Deal Democratic hegemony and the beginning of a new era in American politics. To begin with, Nixon was elected by a Republican Party much changed from that deposed in 1932; and such party metamorphosis has historically brought a fresh political cycle in its wake. . . . This repudiation visited upon the Democratic Party . . . was comparable in scope to that given conservative Republicanism in 1932 for its failure to cope with the economic crisis of the Depression.

—Kevin P. Phillips

We somehow were able to struggle along with the same old complement of judges until a Democrat was elected. Then, and only then, the need for . . . new judges somehow became compelling.

—Rep. Bill Frenzel (R–MN)

The 1968 presidential election ushered in an era of Republican occupation of the White House. Yet this era is distinguished from the two before by the limited sweep of the GOP in other elective offices at the national and subnational levels. The erosion of mass support for the two parties, and the attendant increase in ticket splitting,[1] framed the electoral shackles that dogged the GOP.

The Democratic grip on the Congress from 1969 to 1992 proved to be at least as sturdy as the Republican hold on the Oval Office.[2] This period witnessed the sustained Democratic control of the House of Representatives that commenced in 1955. At the close of the 102d Congress in 1992, Democrats boasted a 100-seat (267–167) majority—20 more than they held at the end of the party's heyday in 1968. Conversely, at the end of the 96th Congress (1968), Democrats enjoyed a 64–36 advantage in the Senate, the key arena for confirmation politics. The 1980 Democratic electoral debacle, however, left 53 Senate seats in the hands of the Republicans. Furthermore, one consequence of the partisan transformation of the upper chamber was transferral of the chair of the Committee on the Judiciary from Edward Kennedy (D–MA) to archconservative Strom Thurmond (R–SC). Six years later control reverted to the Democrats by a 55–45 margin, with stewardship of the Judiciary Committee shifting from Thurmond to Joseph R. Biden (D–DE).

Organizationally, Congress remained more or less the same: with no state being admitted to the Union since 1959, the size of the Senate remained at 100, and House membership was pegged at 435, dating from an apportionment agreement struck by President Hoover with a special session of Congress in 1929.[3] Perhaps the chief institutional change was a host of post-Watergate reform measures in the House that collectively devolved a fair amount of the often autocratic power of committee chairs to subcommittees, and to a lesser extent to the minority party (at least in matters of staff selection).[4] Relatedly, there was dramatic growth in that critical congressional policy resource, staff. Numbering around 7,000 in 1968, congressional staff mushroomed to nearly 18,000 by 1992.[5]

The ability of a president to administer the public's business effectively is critical to the welfare of society and to the former's political fortunes.[6] The contours, structures, and processes of executive management are conditioned by presidential style, and thus vary from administration to administration.[7] Outside of changes in management routines, there were few major changes at the upper echelons of executive organization from 1969 to 1992—the significant ones being the creation of the Departments of Energy and Veterans Affairs, the reorganization of the Department of Health, Education, and Welfare into the Departments of Education and Health and Human Services, and the upgrading of the Bureau of the Budget to the Office of Management and Budget by executive order in 1970.[8] The staff of the Executive Office of the President, an important source of policy advice, grew from under 2,000 in 1968 to almost 3,000 by 1992.[9]

The institutional structure of the judiciary had changed significantly by 1992 as well. The most far-reaching structural alteration was the geographical realignment of the six Deep South states achieved by splitting the Fifth Circuit Court of Appeals into a reconstituted Fifth and a new Eleventh in 1980 (PL 96-452).[10] Additionally, the Court of Appeals for the Ninth Circuit that covered the West Coast, like the Fifth, had experienced such significant judgeship and caseload expansion that it underwent significant internal administrative change. There were also less dramatic changes in court jurisdiction such as creating a new Middle District in Louisiana (PL 92-208) in 1971, reorganizing the district courts of Illinois (PL 95-408) in 1978, and reassigning roving judges to single districts in Alabama (PL 91-272) in 1970, in Washington (PL 95-486) in 1978, in West Virginia (PL 97-471) in 1983, and in Arkansas, Iowa, and Oklahoma (PL 101-650) in 1990.[11] Moreover, this was an age of automation and growth in staff support for the federal courts. By this time the

Administrative Office of the U.S. Courts (created in 1939) and the Federal Judicial Center (formed in 1967),[12] the two major judicial administrative support organizations, were fully in place, and the major legislation involving retirements and benefits had long been passed, albeit with modifications.[13]

The third branch, then, in some respects manifested a degree of continuity analogous to the other two. Yet whereas the trends in institutional growth and voluntary leaving follow patterns benchmarked in the New Deal through the Great Society era carried over into this one, the sheer number of judicial offices and retirements increased to such a staggering extent as to be differences in kind. These dynamics are the centerpiece of this chapter, which focuses on the theme of institutional change during a period of divided government.

Bench Expansion

There were 801 permanent lower federal court judgeships by the end of the Bush administration, 634 on the district courts and 167 on the courts of appeals,[14] an increase in bench size of 85.4 percent since 1968 (see fig. 5.1).[15] Large infusions of new judges through omnibus judgeship bills, rare in the first era and occasional in the second, now became routine. Procedures mandated that the Administrative Office of the United States Courts conduct statistical analyses on caseload pressures and report to the Judicial Confer-

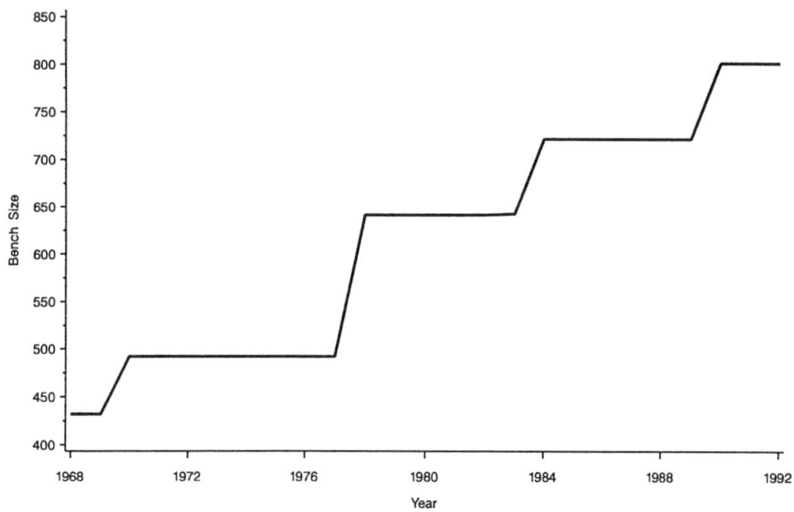

Fig. 5.1. Growth of the federal bench, 1969–92

ence, which in turn makes biennial recommendations to the Congress regarding new positions.[16] Consequently, at least one omnibus bill has been considered by every president dating back to Franklin Roosevelt.

The political wrangling that is intrinsically part of the legislative process is naturally heightened by the prospect of such valued patronage plums as federal judgeships. Although the Judicial Conference and the House and Senate Judiciary Committees are guided by caseload statistics in deciding where to create new positions, only the uninformed would deem these decisions immune from political considerations. The recommendations of the Judicial Conference are, after all, just that. As the Senate—both through the custom of courtesy and the constitutional requirement of confirmation—participates in the selection process with the president, the politics surrounding omnibus bills (which involve the House as well) might be expected to differ under conditions of unified versus divided government. This section chronicles the centrality of new seats to presidential efforts to obtain partisan, if not personal, majorities on the courts under such conditions of government. A detailing of the politics surrounding omnibus judgeship legislation since 1969 illustrates the relationship.

Nixon/Ford Administrations

In September 1968, the Judicial Conference, following its quadrennial survey of judgeship needs on the district courts, recommended 69 additional positions for those courts[17] to complement the recently authorized expansion of the courts of appeals (PL 90-347). Recommended too late in the session to receive consideration, action was deferred to the 91st Congress, where Democrats held sizable majorities of 51 seats in the House and 14 seats in the Senate. With a Republican in the White House control of the government was, of course, divided. What galvanized support for the bill was the inability of Congress to turn its back on unabated increases in caseload. The 1966 omnibus bill proved to be only a palliative; just two years later the Judicial Conference was again calling for additional positions to relieve an overburdened bench.

Congress broke precedent by eventually delivering a bill during a period of divided government, yet the pull of partisan politics dogged the proceedings. S. 952, introduced in and passed by the Senate by voice vote on June 23, 1969, provided for 70 new district court judgeships, the largest bill of its kind ever. Yet in the House, where Democrats held a commanding majority, the number was pared to 57, nine less than the record number awarded Kennedy (PL 87-36). This measure nevertheless sailed through by a vote of 334–20. Ninety-three percent ($N = 181$) of the Democrats voting on the resolution supported it, compared to 96 percent ($N = 153$) of the Republicans. Continuing a trend dating to the 1961 bill, most of those from both parties favoring the legislation came from states targeted for additional judgeships (73 percent Democratic and 71 percent Republican). There were judgeships for the states of the vast majority of the legislators considering the measure, thus making passage virtually assured.[18]

The conference version sent to the president and signed into law (PL 91-272) was a compromise that pegged the number at 64 new positions.[19] In this period of divided government a president did receive an omnibus judgeship bill, mainly because of caseload pressures. New procedures adopted by the Judicial Conference also may have played a role. Following its September 1964 session, the Conference moved from an annual to a quadrennial review of workloads based on alternating surveys of judgeship needs on the appellate and the district courts. Consequently requests for new positions on the courts of appeals alone were made in the March 1967 session, and likewise for the district courts in September 1968. The recommendations were staggered, and made exclusively for one court, but were viewed as half of a comprehensive proposal. Congress, in authorizing new appellate positions in 1968, understood that its district court complement was forthcoming. Moreover, the two parties were no longer divided on the issue of new judgeships as they had often been in the past. Indeed we find substantial majorities of both Democrats and Republicans favoring expansion, sometimes even when there was no position in the offing for the state they represented.[20] Yet the peculiar politics of divided government were nonetheless at work as Democrats focused their efforts on minimizing the number of new positions given to the 37th president. Recall that under unified government during Kennedy and Johnson's presidencies, Congress ultimately authorized a number of judges greater than that recommended by the Judicial Conference, whereas under Nixon the number was lower.

Gerald Ford was not quite so fortunate. Certainly he could argue for more positions on grounds of caseload pressures alone: by 1975, the year Ford's omnibus bill was introduced, caseload increases on the district and circuit courts exceeded those for the three previous administrations, all of which, of course, received additional judgeships. Indeed, in the wake of its quadrennial surveys of staffing needs, the Judicial Conference recommended creating 10 new positions on the appellate courts in its fall 1971 session,[21] and 52 on the district courts one year later.[22] The total climbed to 65 following the September 1974 Conference meeting.[23]

Normally a sympathetic ear for such requests, the Senate Judiciary Committee—while reporting two companion bills (S. 286 and S. 287) for appellate and district court expansion—slashed the levels endorsed by the Conference to 7 and 45, respectively. This time unmoved by caseload arguments, Democrats, who in the 95th Congress held 60 percent of the seats in the

Senate and 67 percent of those in the House, never let the bill get to the Senate floor.[24] The harsh political climate of divided government confronting a caretaker administration weakened by the Watergate malaise, coupled with brightened Democratic prospects for electoral success in the 1976 elections, doomed Ford's judgeship bill. The politics of judgeship legislation once again were getting nasty. Indeed Ford was denied the opportunity to make a single appointment to a new judgeship, something that had not happened since John Tyler's (1841–45) presidency.

Carter Administration

The unabated rise in caseload, the rejection of a bill during Ford's administration, and the unification of government in the hands of the Democrats in 1977 virtually assured enactment of a sizable omnibus bill.[25] Consideration of S. 11 was muddied, however, because the Senate and House versions differed in several controversial respects. On May 3, 1977 the Senate Judiciary Committee reported S. 11, calling for 35 new appellate and 111 new district court judgeships. An amended bill that added two district judges was approved by voice vote by the full Senate on May 24.[26] Judicial Conference recommendations, by comparison, requested 25 new appellate court and 107 new district court positions, again illustrating the influence of unified government on bench expansion.[27] The Senate bill contained a controversial provision to divide the Fifth Circuit into two, with Alabama, Georgia, Florida, and Mississippi forming a new Eleventh Circuit, and Texas and Louisiana comprising a reconstituted Fifth. The extant Fifth suffered from the largest caseload burden in appellate court history, and there was some support for resolving the problem through circuit division.[28] The political pressure from all three branches (especially the judiciary) on this issue that had been building since 1963 now became entangled in a concrete legislative proposal. Circuit splitting was ardently favored by Judiciary Chair James O. Eastland (D–MS), who wanted his state to remain in the Deep South circuit, yet for that very reason the plan was resisted by others concerned about the impact such a division would have on civil rights cases.

One opponent was Peter W. Rodino (D–NJ), who chaired the House Judiciary Committee and its Subcommittee on Monopolies and Commercial Law that evaluated proposals of the Judicial Conference. Rodino expressed serious reservations about the methodology used by the Conference, particularly its projections of future judgeship needs. His subcommittee devised and employed an alternative formula that focused on current rather than future needs, and so arrived at a figure of 34 new appellate and 81 new district court judgeships. At the committee markup sessions on the bill, Rodino proved unable to parry a host of amendments to add positions. The version ultimately reported by the full committee contained only 11 fewer positions than the Senate bill, with the likelihood great of further additions in conference.[29]

The complicating amendment in the House bill involved merit procedures for the selection of judges. Jimmy Carter had pledged in his campaign to appoint judges on the basis of merit rather than political considerations, and a bipartisan House contingent led by Romano L. Mazzoli (D–KY) resolved to hold Carter to his promise. Rodino defeated an amendment to this effect in subcommittee, but to save the bill he lent his support on the floor and so it was included in the House version. The amendment directed that the president should issue regulations "establishing procedures and guidelines for the selection [of judicial nominees], on the basis of merit."[30] The Senate objected throughout to the idea of merit procedures because they potentially hamstrung senatorial prerogatives in the recommendation of nominees from their states.

Public Law 95-486 ultimately authorized 35 new appellate and 117 district judges including four temporary lines, more than twice the record number of positions legislated during Kennedy's term (PL 87-36). The conference committee, after considerable wrangling, omitted the controversial provision to split the Fifth Circuit,[31] adopted a watered-down compromise on merit selection that applied only to district court judgeships, and called upon the president to promulgate merit criteria and procedures. Moreover, the standards were purely voluntary and could be waived by the president by notifying the Senate of his reasons for doing so.[32]

The House vote on the conference bill was 292–112 and, reminiscent of bills of the New Deal era, closely followed partisan lines. Eighty-eight percent of the Democrats in attendance supported the measure (N = 236), whereas 59 percent of the Republicans did not (N = 80). Controlling for whether a judgeship was in the offing, 54 of the 56 Republicans voting for the resolution hailed from states slated to receive additional judges, compared to 228 of 236 for the Democrats. No wonder that Jack Brooks (D–TX) termed the resolution a "classic case" in logrolling that was "a beautiful Christmas tree just spangled with judges"[33] (he nonetheless voted for it).

The Senate vote (67–15) paralleled that in the House. All of the Democrats supported the measure, compared to 52 percent of the Republicans. Breaking down the tally by judgeship locales, 13 of the 15 GOP supporters represented states on the list to receive additional positions, whereas 40 of the 52 Democratic supporters did so. Parenthetically, 11 states received no district judgeships, and 6 of the 15 senators voting "nay" came from one of the deprived states.

Despite the travails over circuit splitting and merit selection controversies, the legislative history of this bill is a paragon of court expansion under unified government. In the face of extraordinary caseload pressures, the Democratically controlled Congress was able to limit bench expansion in the Nixon years, and reject it altogether during Ford's term. Once a compatriot was ensconced in the White House, however, the floodgates opened, leading to the largest single increase in the size of the federal bench ever (and still).

Reagan Administration

President Reagan's judgeship bill was epiphenomenal, being but one element in a comprehensive package that transformed bankruptcy proceedings.[34] The Bankruptcy Act of 1978 (PL 95-598) created a coterie of bankruptcy judges with fixed terms of 14 years who lacked any protection against pay cuts. These Article I judges exercised broad discretionary powers in matters ancillary to bankruptcy matters such as disputes over contracts, landlord-tenant relationships, collective bargaining, antitrust matters, and disputes between parties. Yet with the exception of issues dealing with criminal contempt and injunction, the powers exercised in connection with bankruptcy matters were similar to those historically and constitutionally in the preserve of Article III judges. On June 28, 1982, the Supreme Court nullified PL 95-598 on the grounds that courts exercising such broad powers without the protection of life tenure and salaries threatened the constitutional principle of an independent judiciary.[35] Congress was given until October 4, 1982, to reconstitute the system, a deadline that was extended several times before a new law was approved on June 29, 1984.[36]

To meet the strictures imposed by the High Court, Congress had the option of either reducing the power or increasing the independence of bankruptcy judges. Primarily at the behest of Chair Peter Rodino, the House Judiciary Committee in August reported a bill that would have elevated the complement of 227 bankruptcy judges to the status of Article III district court judges. This approach was favored by bankruptcy judges themselves and leading bankruptcy attorneys, who argued that it would minimize conflicts over jurisdiction. Needless to say, the Justice Department strongly endorsed the Rodino approach. Nevertheless, with the House firmly in the hands of the Democrats,[37] party leaders let the bill die because they did not want to hand President Reagan appointment opportunities of this magnitude.

The Judicial Conference contended that extending Article III status to judges in bankruptcy matters was unnecessary and would create serious administrative problems. The Conference instead proposed that jurisdiction be given to the United States district courts who, in turn, could refer "any or all bankruptcy cases or proceedings to bankruptcy judges." These judges, then, would be officers of the district courts appointed by the respective courts of appeals for terms of 14 years. The Conference ultimately recommended creation of 305 bankruptcy judgeships. Additionally it called for 22 new appellate court positions, and 51 district court judgeships.[38]

Condensing a long and often torturous legislative history, deliberations were stymied by three issues. First, organized labor lobbied heavily for a provision making it more difficult for companies contemplating bankruptcy to abrogate collective bargaining agreements. Second, Congress was divided over a proposal making it harder for consumers to file for bankruptcy. Third, there was considerable resistance to any plan that would reward a Republican president with a shopping basket full of new patronage. Besides the partisan objections of a Democratic majority in the House and a strong minority in the Senate, there were a handful of conservative Republicans (e.g., John East, R–NC) who opposed any expansion of the bench that might aggrandize judicial power and lead to a larger presence in unrelated issues such as busing and school prayer.[39] The final bill (PL 98-353) gave U.S. district courts original jurisdiction over bankruptcy cases, authorizing them to refer narrow issues arising under Title 11 of the U.S. Code to bankruptcy judges, who would be adjuncts of the district courts. Furthermore, the former could withdraw any aspect of a proceeding that had been referred to a bankruptcy judge either unilaterally or on a motion of any party to the proceeding.

The politics of divided government were present in the staffing aspects of the bill, which nonetheless passed by voice vote in both Houses. The bill authorized 232 bankruptcy judges, 73 fewer than called for by the Judicial Conference. Moreover, the president was deprived of these patronage opportunities by a provision that the judges be appointed by the circuit court of each of the 94 judicial districts. Whereas Congress on the one hand mostly followed the recommended list of new positions submitted by the Judicial Conference by authorizing 24 new appellate and 61 district judges,[40] on the outside possibility that a Democrat would be elected president in 1984 the bill mandated that no more than 11 appellate and 29 district positions could be filled prior to January 21, 1985 (the day after Inauguration), on the other.[41]

With the revamping of the bankruptcy system and the attendant workload increase for district judges, it was difficult if not impossible for Democrats to concede some expansion of the bench, especially in light of the recommendations of the Judicial Conference. The politics of divided government nonetheless managed to restrict the degree of increase—in both the short and the long run. The 1984 judgeship bill augmented bench size by only 12.3 percent, significantly less than the increase for Nixon (13.9 percent) and far below the figure for Carter (30.3 percent). Yet caseload increases on the district courts were the highest in percentage terms since the time of the 1961 bill, and the rate of increase on the courts of appeals was the third highest ever. Bench growth during Bush's presidency would be moderated even further.

Bush Administration

At the outset of the 101st Congress, Chief Justice Rehnquist complained that workload pressures and depressed salaries were creating morale problems in the judiciary, impairing the disposition of justice.[42] He requested a salary increase and authorization for 96 additional judges. In this instance workload, measured by new cases filed, indeed had risen at the appeals court level, but had actually declined slightly on the district courts. The latter was attributed largely to decreased filings by the government for defaults on student loans and overpayments in veterans' benefits, and an increase from $10,000 to $50,000 in the minimum amount for a diversity filing. The more litigiously complex cases remained. Of weightier concern was the growing length of time between case filing and disposition, and complaints that the wheels of justice were turning far too slowly (which also drove up litigation costs).[43]

The Senate, led by Judiciary Chair Joseph Biden, responded with a rather bold plan that would set mandatory early trial dates and case tracking. The House took less of a micromanagement approach to judicature. The compromise (H.R. 5316) required each judicial district to establish a local advisory group and devise a delay reduction plan, to make public those cases pending for more than three years, and those either heard or having motions made but awaiting decision for more than six months.[44]

The Democratically controlled Congress had resisted calls of the Judicial Conference for more judges during Reagan's second term, being reluctant, of course, to award the Republican president with a second opportunity to make such choice patronage appointments. Indeed, a bill introduced in March 1987 to add 56 new district court judgeships and 13 on the courts of appeals never made it out of committee, as the Democratic leadership in both Houses stalled the legislation to await the outcome of the 1988 presidential election. Subsequently, midway through George Bush's term in office, Congress was finally compelled to act.

The 1988 and 1990 recommendations of the Judicial Conference called for 20 appellate court and 76 district court positions.[45] H.R. 5316, introduced during the second session of the 101st Congress,[46] however, slashed the total by more than 11 percent to 11 new appellate and 74 district judgeships. Parenthetically, eleven of the judgeships were in districts not recommended for new positions by the Judicial Conference, and four were in districts represented by senators who sat on the Judiciary Committee. Determined to alleviate the backlog in case resolution, the increase in authorized positions was the product of an essentially "put up or shut up" atmosphere: Congress conceded to the Conference's request for staffing relief, yet warned that the burden was now on the judges to get their dockets in order. Like its predecessor, this bill passed by a voice vote in each house of Congress, authorizing the same number of positions (85) given Reagan six years earlier. When seen in light of permanent increases in the lower bench, however, the percentage allocated to Bush was the lowest (11.1 percent) of any judgeship bill from 1969 to 1992.

The Bush measure fits the pattern observed throughout the legislative history of bench expansion. Congress created institutional machinery in the Administrative Office of the United States Courts and the Judicial Conference for the assessment of judgeship needs. Under unified government requests for additional positions are dispatched expeditiously and successfully. When government is divided Congress tends to be more circumspect and inclined toward delay. Yet during the 1969–92 era of divided government, the first branch nonetheless ultimately acceded to the judgeship requests of the Conference, though typically with a smaller complement of positions. Unified government, then, brings not only a speedier response but also a more generous allotment of judgeships to be filled by a president of the same party.

Bench Expansion and Control of Government

The legislative history in the previous section includes one brief (4-year) interlude of unified government; for the remainder of the 24-year era control of the executive and legislative branches of government was divided, although Republicans held a majority of seats in the Senate for six of those years. Of the 1,094 judicial appointments from 1969–92, 369 (33.7 percent) were to new seats. The distribution changes radically depending upon whether the president's party controlled Congress. Under split control, 25.7 percent of the appointments were to new seats, whereas under unified government (Carter's one term), the figure was 59.5 percent (see table 5.1). Excepting President Ford, who was denied an omnibus bill, bench expansion percentages for the Republican presidents are markedly similar (see table 5.2).

An important question in this context is whether the institutional politics of judicial selection are different for appointments to new seats as opposed to replacements.[47] One vantage point from which to examine the question is the ability of administrations to appoint same-party judges. The premise is that when only one position, say a replacement, is at stake, a president can make a preemptive claim for filling that seat with a same-party member. On the other hand, when new seats are created—and in particular when multiple openings occur in a state—presidents find it difficult to deny senators of the opposite party some influence in the selection process. Having to contend with the Senate over a host of policy issues, the White House might be reluctant to jeopardize its entire agenda for the sake of a few appointees.

TABLE 5.1. Sources of Appointment Opportunities

Source	Democrat	Republican
New seats	59.5%	24.8%
Resignations	3.9	4.8
Retirements	27.0	51.5
Elevations	5.8	10.3
Involuntary departures	7.3	8.4

TABLE 5.2. Sources of Appointment Opportunities by President

	Source					
President	New Seats	Resign	Retire	Elevate	Involuntary	Total Appointments
Nixon	29.3%	2.6%	43.1%	10.3%	14.7%	230
Ford	0.0	8.2	65.8	13.7	12.3	61
Carter	59.5	3.9	27.0	5.8	7.3	262
Reagan	24.6	6.0	53.1	9.1	7.3	370
Bush	26.2	3.5	56.4	11.4	2.5	188

The cross-party appointment rate from 1969 to 1992 is 7.7 percent. When broken down by divided versus unified government (which coincidentally is Republican versus Democratic presidents), the figures are 6.8 and 10.5 percent, respectively. Segmenting the data further by replacement versus new seat appointments, we find that 7.0 percent of the time these appointments were made to replacement positions, compared to 9.0 percent for new seats. Although there is only a slight interparty difference in the percentages for replacements (6.7 to 7.1 percent), there is a large discrepancy between parties in appointments to new seats (13.2 to 6.1 percent), especially by level of court. Republicans made no cross-party appointments to the courts of appeals; the rate under Carter is 22.2 percent (in addition to a significantly higher percentage for the district courts). Part of the explanation for the variation lies in the merit procedures Carter used to identify highly qualified nominees regardless of political persuasion. Nevertheless, Carter's omnibus judgeship bill was the largest single expansion of the bench in the nation's history. Perhaps an unnamed source was correct in noting that, "Everyone's been paid off on this thing."[48]

In sum, during this era the federal bench expanded in leaps and bounds. Alternative conditions of government control are instrumental explanations for bench expansion: when the president's party does not hold a majority in Congress, there is less of a chance of omnibus judgeship legislation passing, and the extent of the increase is likely to be smaller in any event. We find some support, on the other hand, for the notion that the politics of the judicial pork barrel vary according to whether the appointments at stake are to fill new or existing positions.[49]

Voluntary Replacements

We observed in the first two eras how the retirement legislation enacted by Congress transformed the third branch, whose members began responding to the opportunities now afforded them. Voluntary turnover, in turn, profoundly influenced the politics of selection. These trends accelerated in the contemporary era. Indeed, the number of judges either resigning, retiring, or opting for senior status between 1969 and 1992 (N = 598) exceeded the total for the previous 180 years (N = 446), that is, dating to the passage of the Judiciary Act of 1789, producing a "crisis in government" according to the Quadrennial Commission of Executive, Legislative and Judicial Salaries.[50] Nearly two out of every three (64 percent) appointments made from 1969 to 1992 were to replace judges who left the bench, making replacement appointments far and away the most important source of staffing.

Further, turnover, large as it was, coincided with the doubling of bench size in a span of two decades. The most important retirement perks were long in place, but with record numbers of judges in service, even a moderate leaving rate meant that more and more would vacate their offices each year,[51] assuring that contemporary presidents would always have a generous number of vacancies to fill. Consequently, attaining or extending partisan majorities on the courts was virtually guaranteed.

The percentage of all vacancies emanating from resignation or retirement was 52.7 percent from 1933 to 1968, an increase of 16 percentage points from the 1869–1932 period. The figure ballooned to 74.4 percent during the modern era, with 67.8 percent coming from retirements and 6.6 percent from resignations. Also during this time the myth of serving for life was challenged by the numbers: less than 12 percent of the judiciary died in office (N = 92), compared to 31 percent (N = 170) in the middle subperiod. Moreover, the mean age of those leaving the bench fell from 72 to 67, as did mean years of service (18 to 15). The judges leaving the bench in record numbers from 1969 to 1992, then, were younger and had shorter careers than their predecessors.

The majority (54 percent) were Democrats, which would be expected given the predominance of Democratic appointees from 1933 to 1968. Regardless of party, the evidence indicates that the decision to leave is affected by political considerations. Judges from 1969 to 1992, as in the two previous eras, tended to leave the bench during a same-party administration. The partisan leaving rate among Democrats, for example, was 66 percent during Carter's presidency. The figure for Republicans, likewise, was 14 percentage points higher when a Republican was president (48 percent).

Table 5.3 provides information on the percentage of resigners and retirees, by party of the judge, and also details mean age and length of service. Table 5.4 organizes leaving cohorts according to appointing president. Almost 60 percent of the voluntary leavers during the Nixon years were Republicans. Whereas the age at leaving for judges of both parties was about the same, Democrats had three years more service at leaving, suggesting they were possibly trying to extend their stay on the bench in hopes that a Democratic

TABLE 5.3. Partisan Leaving Patterns

President	Democratic Leavers	Republican Leavers	Age (Democrats)	Age (Republicans)	Service (Democrats)	Service (Republicans)
Nixon	41.5%	58.5%	68	69	17	14
Ford	61.1	38.9	69	67	15	15
Carter	80.0	20.0	67	64	15	12
Reagan	47.8	51.8	67	67	17	14
Bush	56.6	42.6	69	65	15	15

presidency was on the horizon. The data in table 5.4 are more revealing: 60.4 percent of those who left during Nixon's presidency were originally appointed by Republicans. Seventy-nine Eisenhower appointees, for example, waited for a Republican president before departing the bench.

The picture was far different for Nixon's successor. Less than 40 percent of the leaving cohort during Ford's presidency were Republicans. The low percentage is to some extent tied to the large number of Eisenhower's appointees who left under Nixon. Moreover, most Nixon appointees were relative novitiates to the bench, so there simply was not a sizable reservoir of retirement-ready Republicans in the first place.[52] Even so, 19.2 percent of this group departed under Ford, with an average age (56) and length of service (4 years) understandably far below the other leavers (68 and 15, respectively).

The Carter exiting cohort, by contrast, was overwhelmingly partisan. Eighty percent were Democrats, far and away the highest percentage during the era and one of the largest in the span of the data. They were older, by three years, and had served longer, by the same amount of time, than the GOP contingent leaving under Carter, perhaps indicating an effort to delay departing until a Democrat was in office. Continuing the trend under Nixon, the prominent leaving generation were appointees of Carter's same-party predecessor, Johnson.

The Reagan leaving complement fits the mold: the majority were Republicans, and there was a large GOP generational cohort, in this case Nixon appointees. The partisan composition and generational cohort figures for the group leaving under Bush were similar to Ford's. Republican leavers comprised only 42.6 percent of the total, and the dominant leaving cohort were Carter appointees. Part of the explanation for the low partisan leaving rate is demographic: as was the case with Ford, there was a rather shallow pool of Republican judges of advanced age. Only 24 Nixon and 18 Ford appointees were in active service by the conclusion of Bush's term, at which point 92 percent of all Republicans on the bench were either Reagan or Bush appointees and thus relatively junior. There were, however, 191 (26.7 percent) Democrats in service along with 17 Independents, most of whom were

TABLE 5.4. Generational Leaving Patterns

Leaving President	Appointing President										
	F. Roosevelt	Truman	Eisenhower	Kennedy	Johnson	Nixon	Ford	Carter	Reagan	Bush	Total Same Party
Nixon	2.4%	11.6%	48.2%	12.8%	12.8%	12.2%					60.4%
Ford	4.1	5.5	21.9	31.5	17.8	19.2					41.1
Carter		3.5	6.1	26.3	37.7	20.2	3.5%	2.6%			70.1
Reagan	0.3	1.0	3.4	7.6	22.3	39.2	8.9	8.2	8.9%		60.4
Bush				0.7	9.3	20.5	8.6	39.1	17.9	4.0%	47.0

appointed by Carter. If this historical trend continues then during Clinton's first term the overwhelming majority of leavers should be Democrats appointed by Carter.

Elevations

As detailed in previous chapters, elevations are an interesting and politically astute means of making appointments to the courts of appeals that seem to vary under unified and divided government: when a sitting district judge is elevated, the president is then able to fill the district court vacancy as well, thereby compounding appointments. District court decision making can also be taken into account to maximize selection of nominees compatible with the administration's judicial philosophy or orientation. Finally, district judges tapped for positions on the next court level hold the imprimatur of prior Senate confirmation, an important attribute, especially during periods of divided government.

Elevations as a percentage of all appointments to the courts of appeals rose slightly, from 39.7 percent in the second subperiod to 43.4 percent in the third. This form of appointment was nonetheless far more popular than the percentages suggest. Forty percent (N = 107) of all judges advanced from the district to the circuit courts from 1869 to 1992, for example, were elevated after 1968. Moreover, the annual rate increased steadily over the span of the data, from 2.3 per year from 1933 to 1968 to 4.5 from 1969 to 1992.

There is a striking difference in this means of appointment during periods of unified and divided government. The rate was 22 percentage points greater (48.8 percent) when the president's party did not control Congress from 1969 to 1992, that is, it was roughly two times higher during Republican administrations. Why did Republican presidents employ elevations more than Jimmy Carter, their Democratic counterpart? Was Carter's appointment record to the courts of appeals unusual? We see in table 5.5 that with one exception the partisan appointment rate to the courts of appeals across all subperiods and circumstances of government control is lower for elevations than for appointments from outside the bench. Note that these data ebb when government is politically unified, that is, they move in tandem with periods of bench expansion. Cross-party elevations, then, seem to covary with bench size, implying they might be used as sops to the opposition. Carter's sizable cross-party elevation rate (20 percent) was, from this vantage point, typical rather than exceptional. Indeed, it coincided with the largest expansion of the bench in history.

How does the extent of the partisan pool of district court judges in a given circuit factor into the calculus of elevations? The percentage of the district court bench within the geographical boundary of each circuit sharing the party affiliation of the president was calculated at the time each appellate court appointment was made.[53] If there is a relationship here then elevations

TABLE 5.5. Outside Bench Appointments versus Elevations to the Courts of Appeals

	Same-Party Percentage		District Court Pool	
	Appointments	Elevations	Appointments	Elevations
Overall	94.9%	87.8%	56.4%	65.8%
1869–1932	93.0	83.8	63.2	82.0
Unified	95.6	79.6	61.7	81.1
Divided	88.5	94.7	66.3	84.5
1933–68	98.2	86.3	49.7	62.8
Unified	98.9	86.0	50.6	63.0
Divided	94.7	87.5	45.6	62.4
1969–92	93.8	91.9	58.6	57.5
Unified	85.4	80.0	65.5	62.4
Divided	98.9	94.1	55.4	56.6

should be associated with higher same-party percentages on the district courts and lower percentages otherwise. Table 5.5 shows this to be precisely the case across the entire span of the data, for the first two subperiods, and regardless of whether the president's party governed Congress. The pattern breaks down, however, in the modern era. One possible reason is that contemporary presidents are inattentive to the pool of available district court judges. Alternatively, these data can be mustered in support of the trade-off argument advanced above. Note that the pool percentages decline as the number of additional positions increases. Yet with a large and expanding bench, modern presidents usually have a plentiful cadre of partisans on the district courts available for possible elevation, so they have at their disposal a variety of options for staffing the courts of appeals.

All five presidents from 1969 to 1992 fit the historical mold regarding a higher cross-party appointment rate for elevations than for appointments from outside the bench (see table 5.6). The subperiod departs from the historical

TABLE 5.6. Outside Bench Appointments versus Elevations to the Courts of Appeals (by Administration)

		Same-Party Percentage		District Court Pool	
President	Elevation Rate	Appointments	Elevations	Appointments	Elevations
Nixon	50.0%	100%	91.3%	51.0%	47.3%
Ford	72.7	100	87.5	38.7	49.1
Carter	26.8	85.4	80.0	65.5	62.4
Reagan	41.0	100	96.9	55.4	54.8
Bush	56.8	93.8	95.5	65.5	71.9

relationship between district court pool size, elevations, and off-bench appointments (see table 5.5). The pool percentages for three of the five presidents were roughly equal regarding elevations versus outside the bench appointments; the exceptions are Ford (who was weak politically) and Bush. Indeed during the latter's term the pool for elevations was the largest (71.9 percent) of the five. It simply may be the case that Bush found the relatively young, ideologically appealing, and extensive Reagan cohort of district judges irresistible.[54]

Refining the data further,[55] there is evidence for a government control effect on elevations from 1969 to 1992. Carter was the only president whose party controlled Congress during the era, and his elevation rate is far and away the lowest (see table 5.6). Ford, by contrast, being an unelected president in an age of divided government, assumed office in a precarious political position. Shackled by the Nixon pardoning and the Democrats' overwhelming hold on the 94th Congress, the 38th president was never able to exert much leverage as chief executive. Indeed, selection was problematic at best and limited to 11 appellate court appointments in any case. We can appreciate, then, why Ford's elevation rate dwarfs the others: he apparently felt compelled to send forward to the Senate the names of nominees previously confirmed for district court positions.

The Reagan presidency presents an interesting angle on the elevation phenomenon: for six of these years Republicans held a majority in the Senate, the confirming chamber. We might expect, then, that the rate would shift significantly after the party lost control of that body—being lower during the first three congresses, and higher afterward. Overall, Reagan's elevation rate is lower (41 percent) than all except Carter's, the sole president in this era to serve under unified control. When the data are segmented by the six years in which the Republicans controlled the Senate and the two they did not, the rate of elevations rises from 38.1 to 53.3 percent. The percentages for Nixon and Bush (50 and 56.8 percent) are typical for administrations whose party did not govern the Senate, that is, they are higher than average (44 percent).

One other nuance warrants mention. Presidents tend to select from a particular partisan predecessor's district court cohort in making elevations.[56] The dominant one in three instances (Ford, Carter, and Bush) was the appointing president's immediate partisan predecessor. The chief cohort in the other two (Nixon, Reagan) was the president's own complement of district judges. The Bush cohort stands out: 90 percent of the judges he elevated were appointed to the district court either by Ronald Reagan or by Bush himself. In that Bush and Reagan appointees are similar along a host of demographic and economic dimensions,[57] the current cast on the appellate bench has a face that is distinct even within the universe of Republicans.[58]

Institutional Change

Appointment opportunities arise either from the creation of new positions or from vacancies in existing ones. There are commonalities across administrations from 1969 to 1992, yet they are finely tuned by government control and partisan politics. Each president except Ford received an omnibus judgeship bill during the era, for example, yet Carter's was by far the largest and it was the only one enacted under the condition of unified government. Government control similarly affects the ability of presidents to transform the partisan composition of the bench. The capacity to alter this balance, of course, is to some extent a function of the length of tenure in office, but not exclusively so. Table 5.7 lists, among other things, the annual percentage change in party cohort. The figure for Carter is 3.7 percent, and the average for the others (divided control) is 2.8 percent.

Small percentage point differences translate into significant numbers because of the proliferation in additional judicial offices from 1969 to 1992. Indeed, in the preceding era the average number of appointments per president, for example, was 163, compared to 222 in the third. Standardized in terms of appointments per year, the average in the third subperiod is double that of the second (46 versus 23).[59] Further, voluntary departures—an increasingly significant source of appointment opportunities—take on greater prominence under divided control, comprising 56.3 percent in this regard (see table 5.1), compared to only 30.9 percent under unified government.

The elements of institutional change varied across presidents, but all except Ford realized considerable success in making an imprint on the bench. Moreover, whereas Reagan's mark in this regard has been the subject of considerable fanfare, actually three presidents converted a partisan minority into a majority, a fourth (Bush) extended one, and another (Nixon) nearly attained one. Nevertheless, the case for Reagan being the contemporary court packer is rather impressive. At the time of his inauguration, Republicans occupied under 40 percent of the bench, a figure that had soared to 61.2 percent by eight years later. Perhaps even more striking, Reagan's personal cohort comprised nearly a majority (48.9 percent) of all sitting judges.[60] Indeed he appointed 41 percent more judges than his closest competitor (Carter). Voluntary turnover far more than new positions enabled the 40th president to engineer the largest change in the partisan composition of the bench of the five. The numbers of voluntary leavers (227) and elevations (35) registered during the Reagan years are the largest in the history of the lower federal courts, and of course so are the numbers appointed.

The Bush administration followed the contours established by its predecessor. His appointments came largely from voluntary turnover, and were second only to Reagan's, percentage-wise. Even so, Bush was far less effective

TABLE 5.7. Institutional Change

President	Partisan Appointment Rate	Party Cohort, Start of Term	Party Cohort, End of Term	Average Annual Change in Party Cohort	Personal Cohort, End of Term	Overall Change[a]
Nixon	95.7%	29.8%	49.5%	3.3%	43.3%	49.3%
Ford	90.9	49.5	54.2	2.4	13.0	15.6
Carter	83.9	45.8	60.4	3.7	41.3	43.6
Reagan	98.7	39.6	61.2	2.7	48.9	55.5
Bush	94.7	61.2	72.2	2.8	25.0	28.4

[a]Appointments from new seats, retirements, resignations, elevations, and involuntary turnover/size of bench at end of administration.

in transforming the bench. At the conclusion of his presidency there were more than 100 unfilled vacancies, thus paving the way for his Democratic successor to erase the GOP majority on the lower federal courts.[61] It is nonetheless striking that by the end of 1992 over 70 percent of all sitting judges were Republicans. Moreover, if the Reagan and Bush judges are considered as one cohort, they comprised two out of every three (68.5 percent) judges on the bench in 1992.

Nixon in some respects was nearly as successful as Reagan in packing the courts.[62] Falling short of leaving the bench in Republican hands at his departure, he nonetheless managed to alter the partisan balance by nearly 20 percentage points. Like Reagan and Bush, the bulk of Nixon's appointments came from a slew of retirements, as well as from an omnibus judgeship bill that was rather generous for a president serving under divided government. Ford's brief stint as essentially a caretaker president in a situation of divided government is reflected in the almost negligible impact he had on the bench, except to push the GOP percentage over the top into majority status.[63]

Sandwiched between two pairs of Republican presidents, Jimmy Carter converted a modest Republican majority on the bench to a comfortable Democratic predominance by the time he left office. This would not have been possible without the largest omnibus judgeship bill in the history of the federal judiciary. The result of this massive infusion of new positions was an alteration of the partisan balance by 15 percentage points.[64] Almost 60 percent of Carter's appointments were to new positions, more than twice the figure of all of his GOP counterparts. Carter's average annual change in partisan cohort (table 5.7) was the highest among the five. The Carter complement has been durable—comprising 41.3 percent of the bench in 1980, and declining only to 23.7 percent twelve years later.

The seeds of the patterns in bench transformation observed in the contemporary era were sown in the first era and germinated in the second. As such, the modern period was marked by continuity. Yet by the 1990s the size of the bench eclipsed that of the Congress; its members left in record numbers, belying the tradition of lifetime service; and its partisan composition now changed swiftly and routinely. All institutions change over time, but from 1969 to 1992, the long run essentially became the short run. The lesson of the modern era is that abrupt change is now the norm rather than the exception.

CHAPTER 6

An Institutional Behemoth?

> The first proposition is to establish a new place of holding court; the next is to create a new district with a district judge, marshal, and attorney; the next step is to build a courthouse-post office; and if this system has to go on . . . we shall have in the United States as many places of holding courts as there are counties, and instead of having sixty or seventy district judges you will have six or seven hundred.
>
> —Senator Lyman Trumbull (D–IL), 1872

> I want you to make me one promise. . . . The only thing I would like for you to do is to keep in mind the problem that we have with judges when they get too old. When you've served your time and have gotten to the point where you should retire, retire. . . . That's the best way to keep the judiciary functioning properly.
>
> —District Judge Adrian A. Spears, paraphrasing Lyndon B. Johnson

In chapter 2 we presented an overview of the historical transformation of the judiciary, and then examined those dynamics in detail in three distinct partisan eras. At this point we step back to gain a wide-angle picture of the dynamics across the scope of the study. We employ this format by summarizing the degree to which particular subperiods conform to or depart from historical patterns. Following that, we place our findings in the context of the literature on institutionalism. With membership now approaching a millenary, a rather lively debate—both on and off the bench—has been joined over the question of how large the third branch can become and still function effectively. We examine the contending points of view, and offer some observations on the possible consequences of unabated expansion for judicial socialization and institutional stability.

Historical Overview

Variations on a Theme

Table 6.1 details the degree to which the three subperiods we investigated deviated from the historical means of institutional change and its components.

TABLE 6.1. Historical Change

	Overall	Period 1	Period 2	Period 3
New seats[a]	4.7%	4.7%	4.5%	5.1%
Democrat	4.7	2.4	5.0	12.5
Republican	4.7	5.5	2.8	3.6
Elevations[b]	43.1	42.6	39.9	49.1
Democrat	32.9	21.4	40.1	29.2
Republican	49.5	49.7	39.2	53.1
Voluntary turnover[c]	5.6	4.6	5.5	8.5
Democrat	4.9	3.8	5.2	7.3
Republican	6.1	4.9	6.6	8.7
Same-party leaving rate[d]	60.1	63.5	54.7	59.1
Democrat	51.6	36.1	57.2	74.7
Republican	65.5	72.7	46.0	55.9
Institutional change[e]	16.3	16.8	15.3	16.6
Democrat	15.4	13.6	15.4	22.8
Republican	16.9	17.9	15.1	15.3

[a]Appointments to new seats/bench size.
[b]Elevations/appellate court appointments.
[c]Resignations + retirements/bench size.
[d]Same-party voluntary turnover/resignations + retirements.
[e]Total appointments/bench size.

The information is provided overall, by subperiod, and by party occupying the White House.[1] The importance of bench expansion to institutional change is showcased in the contemporary era. Whereas the historical average (4.7 percent) is below the period norm (5.1 percent), the explosion in bench size since 1968 is actually understated. Calculated as the proportional increase in this regard, with uninterrupted growth from 1869 to 1992, increases of the past 24 years translate into substantially larger ones than in earlier times because the base becomes larger from one era to the next. Across the board there are marked differences by party, which in turn conform to the politics of partisan control of the institutional reins of government: unified control is fertile soil for the creation of new seats—for the Republicans in the first era (5.5 percent), and the Democrats in the second (5.0 percent) and third (12.5 percent).

The contribution of voluntary departures to institutional change, again relative to bench size, takes precedence in the second period (5.5 percent) and crests in the third (8.5 percent). Historically, this is the main driver of membership recomposition. The long-term effects of the retirement options enacted in the first period are displayed in bold relief: the mean for the second period (5.5 percent) is 20 percent higher than the mean for the first, and for the third (8.5 percent) it is 55 percent greater than the second. Also note the growth in voluntary departures during Republican administrations, from 4.9

percent in the first era, to 6.6 percent in the second, and 8.7 percent in the third. The percentages for Democrats follow the same pattern but the percentages are lower.

Leaving the bench voluntarily is to a great extent a function of opportunity. The lofty percentages for the GOP in the first period are somewhat deceptive: the retirement option was limited for much of the era but the timing of the legislation greatly favored Republican administrations, who dominated appointment politics from 1869 to 1932. The high mean (72.7 percent) derives from there being a Republican in the White House 75 percent of the time, whereas the substantially lower Democratic score (36.1 percent) devolves from the sparse number of Democrats—senior or otherwise—on the bench during the Cleveland and Wilson years.

Likewise in the second era the Republican (Eisenhower's) figure is lower (46 percent) precisely because GOP jurists had not been appointed in any number for over twenty years. Carter's election in the third era, by contrast, came only eight years after an extended period of Democratic control, so there was a sizable cohort of Democrats on the bench, many of whom were now eligible for senior status.

The elevation rate—another component of institutional change—is highest in the third (49.1 percent) and first (42.6 percent) eras, during which times the GOP dominated the executive branch. Politics in the first era in general, and specifically appointments to the district bench, took on a distinctly Republican cast, producing a 28 percentage point spread between the Republican (49.7 percent) and the Democratic (21.4 percent) elevation rates. Remarkably, in the ensuing 1933–68 era of Democratic control, Eisenhower's score (39.2 percent) is only slightly below the Democratic mean (40.1 percent). Coming full circle, Republican administrations in the past 24 years have collectively registered record elevation rates (53.1 percent), and the gap between the two parties is also the widest ever.

As shown in chapter 5, the majority of those elevated by Ronald Reagan and George Bush were also their appointees to the district bench. Jimmy Carter, however, was disinclined to elevate, in part because the previous generation of Democratic district judges (Kennedy and Johnson appointees) were advanced in age when the trend was to select younger nominees. Further, Carter brought with him to the Oval Office a pledge to diversify the bench by race, ethnic origin, and gender. Few nontraditional judges sat on the district courts when he entered office, however,[2] forcing him often to go outside the bench to identify recruits. The administration's elevation rate (29.2 percent) for these reasons is among the lowest in the span of the data.[3]

Whereas the extent of institutional change is fairly consistent across subperiods, ranging from 15.3 to 16.8 percent, the magnitude of recomposition is growing due to increasing bench size. Republican presidents have had a larger impact on transforming the courts, but their ability to do so is again aided by opportunity, that is, by the frequency of same-party control of the White House. Evidentially, some strategizing is also involved. Republican percentages in the middle era (15.1 percent), for example, approximate those for Democrats (15.4 percent), even while the latter dominated appointment politics. Nevertheless, the rate for Carter (22.8 percent) is the highest in the distribution, attributable largely to the 1978 omnibus judgeship bill, whereas the percentage for his Republican counterparts during the third era was nearly 50 percent lower (15.3 percent) when calculated by congress.

Excepting voluntary turnover, indicators of institutional change and its components, then, are rather stable over time. There are notable interparty differences: Democrats are increasingly prone to rely on new positions in making appointments, whereas Republicans rely on replacements from voluntary turnover and elevations. The root of these varying staffing methods can more often than not be traced to a structural feature of politics, unified government.

Bench Expansion and Voluntary Turnover

Analysis of historical time series such as those studied here is facilitated by methodology developed by Box and Jenkins that is both well known to and widely employed by social scientists.[4] The technique permits a determination of whether and how longitudinal data are affected by time and by values within the time series. This information is used, in turn, to model empirical relationships.

We are especially interested in the role that bench expansion and voluntary departures play in appointment politics. Correlations of these data with time, and between and among series observations are readily available from any number of time-series programs. These statistics inform us of any significant variation or movement over time. We can then decide whether the data trend or not—and how best to incorporate and control for it if they do. Likewise, we can observe whether observations in a time series are related to or independent of one another as required. Knowing the serial structure of the series helps us to model correctly its relationship to other time series of interest. We can see how associations change under different conditions and determine whether variation in the value of government control, for example, has an instantaneous ("zero order") or a delayed effect. We can identify the nature of the effect, that is, whether it is temporary or permanent. This ability to develop, model, and evaluate easily and reliably a variety of longitudinal relationships no doubt accounts for the popularity of the Box-Jenkins approach.

Following the discussion of the dynamics of institutional change, we expect to find a significant association of unified versus split political control of government with both bench expansion and voluntary turnover. We anticipate that the number of new judicial positions, for instance, will increase sizably during periods when the president's party governs Congress. We expect that caseload will condition the relationship. Republican administrations should be linked to somewhat higher rates, historically, because of the extent of court restructuring and bench growth in the first era, one that comprised over half the length of the period of study.

In previous chapters we documented the explosive growth in voluntary departures between 1869 and 1992, and established the tendency of judges to leave under an administration governed by their party. Combining the two, a model of partisan turnover that incorporates political (same-party control of the Senate, party occupying the White House) and corporate (caseload, pay raises, improved retirement benefits) aspects is developed.

The data are segmented by congress, so there are 62 observations for each variable. Bench expansion is the percent increase in the number of judgeships from one congress to the next. Voluntary departures indicates the ratio of same-party leavers to the total number retiring or resigning. Unified government, Senate control, and party of the president are measured as 1 = unified government, majority in the Senate, Democrat in the White House, and 0 = otherwise. Caseload is calculated by taking the average of the change in the number of filings in both the district and appeals courts. Congresses during which salaries increased 10 percent or retirement benefits were upgraded are coded 1, and 0 otherwise.

Table 6.2 reports the results of this investigation. Over the course of the 41st through 102d Congresses, bench growth averaged nearly 5 percent per congress. Caseload increases at first glance seem to be only marginally related to the proportional rise in positions. Indeed, the estimates show that for every 1 percent rise in caseload, the bench grew by only 0.04 percent. We need to keep in mind, however, that it was not unusual for filings to increase anywhere from 15 to 30 percent[5] from 1869 to 1992, meaning that the cumulative effect is larger than it seems. The analyses reveal that political conditions, nevertheless, largely dictated the pace of expansion. The rate of bench growth nearly doubles (9.1 percent), for example, during periods of unified governance. Further, historically, when a Democrat sits in the White House bench growth is on average 3 percent lower. Modern trends notwithstanding, the party control effect of unified government is attributable to extraordinary expansion rates during Republican administrations of the 1869 to 1932 era spanning 32 congresses. During this uncommonly lengthy period of Republican hegemony it was not unusual to see a 10 percent increase or more in the size of the bench, whereas that for Democrats was typically either nil or marginal.[6]

Partisan voluntary turnover averages 60 percent per congress. There is a substantial increase (16.9 percent) during years of same-party control of the Senate, offset by an even larger decrease when a Democrat is president (−18.1 percent). The lower percentages for Democrats come from their having fewer opportunities than Republicans from 1869 to 1992 to retire or resign

TABLE 6.2. Time-Series Analysis of New Positions and Voluntary Turnover, 1869–1992 (by Congress)

	New Positions	Voluntary Turnover
Average	4.7%	60.1%
Unified government	4.4[a]	—
	2.2	
Senate majority	—[b]	16.9[a]
		(9.0)
Party of the president	−3.0[c]	−18.1[a]
	(2.1)	(5.4)
Caseload	.04[c]	6.9[a]
	(.03)	(4.2)
Raise	—[b]	3.1
		(3.1)
Retirement peaks	—[b]	8.6[b]
		(4.8)

[a]Significant at the .10 level, one directional test (standard errors in parentheses).
[b]Variable not included in analysis.
[c]Significant at the .05 level, one directional test (standard errors in parentheses).

during an administration governed by their party (32 percent). As for corporate influences, both caseload (6.9 percent) and enhanced retirement benefits (8.6 percent) spur departures. Raises, often advocated as the means of lengthening tenure on the bench, by contrast, do not dampen turnover, which is actually understandable in many cases. After all, those considering senior service, for example, could look forward to significantly lower workloads while being entitled to any pay hikes legislated for their full-time colleagues. Given the circumstances, there is little incentive to stay.

In sum, regardless of the particular lenses used to scrutinize the data—be they historical overviews, in-depth treatments of subperiods, or analysis of time series—there is unmistakable evidence for the importance of divided or unified government in making permanent structural changes in the judiciary. Yet the historical transformation of the bench is on balance an interinstitutional phenomenon that includes Congress in the case of bench expansion, and the judiciary itself for voluntary turnover.

The Institutional Basis of Judicial Change

In a seminal essay on the institutionalization of the U.S. House of Representatives,[7] Nelson W. Polsby stipulates three characteristics of an "institutionalized organization":

1. it is relatively well-bounded, that is, it is differentiated from its environment and its members are identifiable;

2. it is complex, that is, there is a specialization of labor, and its parts are not wholly interchangeable even though they might be interdependent; and
3. it tends to follow universalistic rather than particularistic criteria, that is, precedents and roles are followed and impersonal codes displace personal preferences as standards of behavior.[8]

Although the third branch is arguably the one most permeable to political intrusion by the other two,[9] it clearly satisfies Polsby's criteria. Since 1869, however, its complexion and institutional environment have changed—sometimes in fell swoops, other times by events mutating its course of evolution. This can be observed in all of its dimensions. The *organization* has been transformed, illustrated by the creation of the courts of appeals in 1891, and to a lesser degree by the proliferation of judicial districts and court restructuring over time. So have its administrative *rules and processes,* as evidenced by the creation of the Judicial Conference in 1922 and its subsequent influence on bench expansion. The same is true for the judiciary's *informal norms,* as in the case of the ever-growing prevalence of politically timed voluntary departures. In this section we return to several of the themes introduced in the first chapter to see how the results of this study comport with institutional approaches to political analysis.

Institutional Change

We consider our findings to be a rather stunning affirmation of the importance of same-party control of the first and second branches, and endorse the sentiment expressed by Sir John Robert Seeley over a century ago: "History is past politics, and politics present history."[10] The cycles witnessed in electoral politics[11] carry over to the staffing of the third branch. Although virtually all presidents since the Civil War have left an imprint on the partisan composition of the bench, the condition of government structure (unified or divided control) leveraged the degree of change. The makeup of the "tool box" (strategies for staffing the bench) also hinged on the presence or absence of partisan unity.

Bench Expansion

Prior to 1922, expansion of the bench was a gradual process in which except in rare instances the creation of judgeships was legislated on a case by case, bill by bill basis.[12] The establishment of the Judicial Conference by the Act of 1922, which made it the initiator or agenda setter[13] for enlargement of the third branch, marks the institutionalization of a process that subsequently would produce regular, abrupt, and often massive changes in bench size in the form of omnibus judgeship bills. The Conference has come to play not only this role but also one of "expert" on judgeship needs and judicial administration in general. A prominent vein in the bureaucratic politics literature details how the expertise of policy professionals in the executive branch can be translated into political influence,[14] a lesson that should not be lost on students of the judiciary.

Bench expansion, then, is an interinstitutional phenomenon in which all three branches of the federal government participate, yet it is one that is conditioned by institutional norms and processes.[15] We have documented the fact that omnibus legislation is more likely to be enacted when the president's party governs Congress and that the number of additional positions is likely to be greater in this case than the total recommended by the Judicial Conference. Appointment politics to some extent also hinge on government control: cross party appointments tend to occur when judicial patronage is increased during periods of expansion.[16]

Voluntary Departures

Through various and sundry legislation enacted since 1869, Congress made early exit from the bench an attractive option, one that jurists have been willing not only to exercise, but also to time politically. We find that partisan turnover, in turn, covaries with the degree of same-party control of the Senate. Thus, an institutional change authorized by Congress stimulated a neo-institutional response on the part of the judiciary. Perhaps the major beneficiary has been the White House, because it was given the opportunity to replace the droves of leavers. Indeed as we observed, historically—and especially in the contemporary era—filling vacancies is the preeminent means by which presidents place their stamps on the bench.

Filling vacancies, or for that matter new seats, is of course an institutional process shared by the president, who nominates, and the Senate, which confirms. Yet certain norms have evolved around the "advice and consent" provision of Article II, Section 2, most notably the custom of courtesy. We found evidence of another arrangement between the two: the same-party appointment rate is higher for filling vacancies than for new seats. This suggests that interbranch appointment politics, in particular the influence of senatorial courtesy, in part depend upon whether or not the pool of patronage is being enlarged.

Elevations

Our interest in elevations is sparked because it is a politically efficient means of staffing the appellate bench, and one that is growing in popularity. The cost-benefit margin afforded presidents seeking to make elevations is made more attractive by several features of the institutional setting of confirmation. Presidents, for one, limit failed confirmations as district judges have already survived one round of hearings.[17] Presumably, then, the onus is on the Senate, which, barring new questions since the first go-round, would place itself in the position of second-guessing itself if it wanted to block the elevation to the courts of appeals.

By filling appellate positions this way rather than going outside the bench, presidents have the opportunity of observing the behavior of potential nominees in a pertinent institutional setting. By then using track record as a selection criterion, presidents can appease senators of the opposition party while still sending up nominees who comport with their policy aspirations. We found evidence of this in the higher cross-party appointment rates for elevations. Their prominence as an appointment tactic is similarly a function of unified versus divided government and the partisan composition of the district bench. Elevations are more likely to be made when government is divided, for the above reasons. They also are related to the opportunity structure of the pool: elevations covary with the percentage of the potential pool that shares the president's party label.

At the start of this chapter and in chapter 5, we noted that the elevation rate pegged out in the contemporary era. We also ventured that with the proliferation of bench growth during this time, a point may have been reached where presidents will always be able to identify a number of compatible district court judges to advance to the next level. If so then we would expect continued acceleration in the elevation rate as we approach the twenty-first century. If that occurs, and assuming the tendency of recent presidents including Bill Clinton to promote judges of the courts of appeals to the High Court, the third branch might be evolving toward a new conception of the judicial career.[18] With retirement benefits based upon years of service, the third branch already exhibits some traits of the career bureaucracy in the executive branch. The possible implications of this hypothetical shift are difficult to foresee. One might be a further differentiation or specialization of roles and functions, and more durable expectations of leadership advancement within the judicial hierarchy, both of which Polsby saw as a defining characteristic of institutionalization.[19]

We would also expect judicial socialization to take a firmer hold, again with unpredictable consequences. On the one hand, enhanced socialization might advance adherence to a particular set of professional and decisional standards, both on and off the bench, adding to the stability and uniformity of case law across districts and circuits. On the other hand, certain individuals and groups in the political system might view this development negatively. We suspect some would have reservations about a countermajoritarian (that is, appointive) bench for which lateral entry is the exception rather than the norm. In this sense the alternative formulation of the judicial career very well could suppress diversity in the points of view of those who wear the ermine by limiting legal advancement to those who work their way through the ranks. This outcome would be especially telling for groups beginning to make inroads in mobilizing politically and diversifying elective institutions such as the Congress, but who would then have to start at the bottom of the judicial hierarchy and endure—perhaps for years or even decades—underrepresentation on the appellate bench.

1,000 Judges before the Year 2000?

> The federal judiciary is undergoing a basic transformation. While the change has many causes, the most profound has been the phenomenon of growth both in jurisdiction and in personnel. It is not possible to point to one defining event . . . [r]ather, the course of expansion has been gradual and incremental. . . . The time has arrived, however, to begin looking at the forest instead of just the trees. When the cumulative impact of recent developments is considered, it becomes clear that the basic character of an important public institution has been altered. (Circuit Judge J. Harvie Wilkinson III)[20]

As discussed in chapter 5, in the consideration of the 1990 omnibus judgeship bill several senators, notably Judiciary Committee Chair Joseph Biden (D–DE), were disgruntled: even though Congress in the past had granted the Judicial Conference's request for more judges, the administration of justice had not improved. He and others complained especially about the increasing delays in the disposition of cases. Biden decided that it was high time to take a closer look at federal judicature, including the way in which the Judicial Conference arrived at its recommendations for new judgeships.

The Senate Judiciary Committee Report that accompanied the bill was rather critical of the criteria and process used by the Conference in making its assessments, especially because no weighted caseload system was used in developing recommendations for the appellate courts, which "makes any realistic evaluation next to impossible."[21] The committee was also troubled that appeals court recommendations "appear[ed] to be driven more by the specific requests made by circuit judicial councils than by hard, factual analysis."[22]

As a result, Title II of the Judicial Improvements Act of 1990 directed the General Accounting Office, the auditing and investigating arm of Congress, to study the procedures used by the Judicial Conference in deriving its judgeship lists. The GAO expressed similar concerns about the rationality of the process:

> We found that the Conference's recommendations for 29 (53 percent) of the 55 districts could be justified using the written guidelines, while recommendations for the remaining 26 (47 percent) could not. . . . For reasons that were not clear, the Conference appeared to accept some districts' justifications as reasons to support judgeship requests but reject those same justifications when used by other districts.[23]

This episode occasioned a good bit of soul searching—both on and off the bench—over the questions of how effective the omnibus approach to bench expansion was, and whether there was an outer limit beyond which the overall size of the bench would be dysfunctional to the administration of the federal courts.

Apart from the methodology employed by the Judicial Conference, some are concerned with the very nature of the omnibus approach that periodically jolts the system with huge infusions of new members. Given what we know about the relevance of unified government for bench expansion, critical judgeship needs can go unmet for years until the political conditions are ripe. By that time, judicial administration has deteriorated and the new judges consequently become a palliative for, rather than a solution to, the problem.[24] Additionally, with omnibus bills, the president's efforts in identifying nominees and the Senate confirmation process can become overloaded and/or excessively politicized, thereby creating further delays (as witnessed in the excess of 100 unfilled positions at the close of the 102d Congress). In effect, the judiciary is placed in the position of always having to play catch-up.

The delays generate a host of problems. An organization must be able, to some extent anyway, to inculcate its new members to their roles (both ethical and organizational), responsibilities, and rules for maintaining the courts as effective organizations. New members need the opportunity to become acculturated to their new colleagues and administrative staffs, and to develop productive routines and relationships.[25] These problems are especially acute for the courts of appeals, which of course are collegial courts,[26] but are present as well on the district courts, which are collections of equals rather than hierarchically organized entities. The potential problem is that the practice of enlarging the courts in fits and starts rather than through an orderly process of planned change undermines the judicial socialization process.

While these concerns usually surface in the context of bench expansion, they are exacerbated by the recent acceleration in voluntary departures. Moreover, since the seventies there has been considerable delay in filling vacancies, which, in turn, burdens the active judges and in some cases creates morale problems. New members, regardless of whether their appointments are to fill vacancies or new positions, must be integrated into the organization. The irony of the situation is that

> As the rate of regeneration [institutional change] increases the proportion of members who do know the local scene declines, while the proportion of members who need that information increases. Socialization therefore should consume a greater portion of the total activity of the organization.[27]

The task of socializing new members is an administrative cost, not only in terms of acclimating them to their new positions, but also by involving larger initial efforts in coordination and conflict resolution, so "[i]f the administrative load increases, the ratio of administrative activities to other activities expands."[28] Turnover and continual bench expansion, then, can create a dysfunctional administrative syndrome.

Concerns over the consequences of unabated growth certainly are not new to the 1990s. Forty years ago Justice Felix Frankfurter argued that

> . . . inflation of the number of district judges. . . . will result, by its own Gresham's law, in a depreciation of the judicial currency and the consequent impairment of the prestige and of the efficacy of the federal courts.[29]

The debate over capping the size of the judiciary has found its way into the inner sanctum of the Judicial Conference meeting room, and beyond that some of the judges are starting to go public.

Early in 1993, two appeals court judges engaged one another on the Op-Ed page of the *New York Times* on the question, "Are 1,000 Federal Judges Enough?"[30] Judge Jon O. Newman of the Second Circuit took the affirmative position.[31] He argued first of all that unlimited growth would diminish the quality of appointees and this, coupled with a threat to the integrity of the Senate confirmation process that would collapse under its own weight, would lead to a mediocre bench. Unrestrained growth would also overbureaucratize the judiciary and jeopardize the collegiality and efficiency of the courts of appeals, which work in panels.[32] The quality of the law would suffer as well. Historically, he claimed, as the judiciary grows so too does caseload, and this would require judges to adopt shortcuts (e.g., less oral argument and fewer published opinions). Additionally, unchecked growth would lead to the creation of either more districts and circuits or alternatively enormous increases in the number of judges per court. In either case the result would be a further fragmentation in the coherence of federal law.[33]

> America faces a crucial choice that will determine whether the Federal court system continues to serve its historic function or slowly deteriorates into a vast faceless bureaucracy. . . . Like global warming, the

> ever-growing Federal bench poses a problem that we may not recognize until it is too late. I hope Americans in 2030 will not ask, "How could those in charge back in the 1990s have let the Federal judiciary grow so large that it is no longer worth having."[34]

Judge Stephen Reinhardt of the Ninth Circuit offered the rejoinder,[35] arguing that what is actually needed is a sizable increase in the number of judges. The quality of jurists will not have to decline, as there is an abundant supply of qualified lawyers in the legal system. Reinhardt believes that the larger danger is that capping the bench and thus the number of cases heard will limit court access for the poor, minorities, women, and other disadvantaged persons. With Congress passing more and more laws affecting more and more people, there simply is no alternative to increasing the number of judges to reconcile disputes over the legislation. He also takes issue with Judge Newman over the implications of a larger judiciary for the quality of justice: the quality of justice is already deteriorating because there is a judicial shortfall, which has led to shortcuts in decision making and increased bureaucratization. The answer is more judges:

> Our nation must decide what kind of Federal judicial system it will have. Should it be large enough to serve all people whose basic rights are threatened? Or should it be a precious jewel that primarily provides a forum for the resolution of important commercial disputes? What is the purpose of Federal courts anyway? To serve the privileged or the many?[36]

Three times before there was controversy over the method or the magnitude of omnibus expansion of the bench. Recall that in the 1930s Republicans challenged the proposed omnibus increase in the judiciary during the Roosevelt administration, to no avail of course. Democrats returned the favor during the late 1950s when the caseload-based methodology used by the Judicial Conference to determine additional judgeships was challenged in the Senate, stalling tactics that successfully prevented the Eisenhower administration from receiving a second omnibus bill. The Democrats did so once again when House Judiciary Committee Chair Peter Rodino took issue with the means by which the Conference developed its projections of future judgeship needs, though of course the bill ultimately succeeded. The Conference can expect its 1993–94 recommendations, and the methodology used to arrive at them, to receive a heightened degree of scrutiny—although this time it will probably come from the Republicans.

In fact at its March 1993 meeting the Judicial Conference turned the issue over to its Long Range Planning Committee for investigation.[37] Six months later, with the recommendations of the Planning Committee in hand, the Conference had a "fairly long" discussion of a proposal to set a maximum number on the size of the judiciary.[38] Ultimately it decided to: "Reaffirm its previous position favoring a relatively small Article III Judiciary but opposing any efforts to set a maximum limit on the number of judgeships."[39] Even so, the recommended number of additional positions submitted to the 103d Congress, 34, of which 29 are temporary, is the smallest requested increase in the last 45 years.[40] Whereas the number of new offices requested by the Judicial Conference in its September 20, 1994, report crept up to 43 (25 temporary and 3 conversions), the Conference appears to be taking a middle-of-the-road course by rejecting capping, and so affirming its prerogative to be the initiator of judicial expansion, but proposing modest increases in bench size during this period of scrutiny.

The Republican takeover of Congress following the 1994 elections does not bode well for additions to the judicial workforce during the remainder of Clinton's first term, at which point six years will have passed since the last judgeship bill. Depending upon the outcomes of the 1996 presidential and congressional contests, one can forecast either a return to the traditional format of unrestrained growth and the attendant patronage in a period of unified government, or continued gridlock on the issue of allocating additional positions if the condition of divided government continues.

The question of how large the bench should be cannot be answered in the abstract, but instead must be related to the issue of how justice can best be administered by the federal courts.[41] The issue of caps on the size of the bench, nonetheless, persists. It remains to be seen how far administrative reforms can go toward redressing a situation that is driven, at least in part, by a Congress that has ensured a steady demand in judicial business by its enactment of complex regulatory and protective legislation. Judge Wilkinson, for one, believes that Congress ought to look in a different direction as a way to stem judicial growth:

> [T]he tendency in Congress has often been to respond to a problem by providing a federal cause of action for it. More judges are then needed to meet the jurisdictional needs, and with more judges provided, Congress in turn feels justified in expanding further the scope of federal jurisdiction. With expanded jurisdiction there comes a need for still more judges. And so on, and so forth.[42]

As an alternative, Carl Baar, in a report prepared for the Federal Judicial Center,[43] urged that an annual maximum increase in the number of new positions be mandated by Congress. In his view the number should be no larger than eight, and where they would be assigned would be determined by the Judicial Conference. Yet Baar himself acknowledged that the political support for retaining the omnibus approach is formidable:

> The problem is that these pleas have little weight when compared with the support generated for an omnibus judgeship bill at the beginning of a new administration. The present system encourages the development of an inflationary psychology: secure as many judgeships as possible to protect the converging interests of executive, legislative and judicial branches against an uncertain future.[44]

In chapter 1 we discussed how institutions impart norms, rules, and order to individual behavior. These in turn guide institutional evolution, providing a set of relatively stable expectations to individuals and other organizations with which the institution interacts in the larger environment. Perhaps no other governmental institution was so consciously formulated for stability and continuity as the third branch. Elsewhere[45] we demonstrated how significant departures from precedent destabilize the judiciary, at least in terms of stoking the rate of voluntary departures. The continual infusion of new judges—through omnibus judgeship bills and increases in voluntary leaving—cannot help but undermine the possibility for paced evolution and socialization, and exacerbate institutional stress. During the 1970s and 1980s, a series of reports prepared by the Commissions on Executive, Legislative, and Judicial Salaries told of a crisis in government signified by increasing turnover and shortened periods of service brought on by artificially depressed salaries. The true crisis, we contend, is not the underpayment of federal judges, for the vast majority are well off,[46] but the serious undermining of their institution through enormous increases in new members, often of very different political/ideological persuasions, coupled with record-shattering annual departures and declining length of service.

The incentives to leave and the propensity to expand the judicial patronage list transpired gradually for much of the 1869–1968 era. The floodgates opened afterward. Congress managed to take an institution that was 20 percent smaller than itself in 1968 and transform it into an institutional behemoth 50 percent larger than Congress only two decades later. Turnover that was moderate and manageable in 1960 quadrupled 30 years later as judges responded in ever-growing numbers to the perks of retirement. A lesson of a study of the modern bench is that abrupt change in an institution of once limited size, whose members often served until death, is now the norm rather than the exception.

The continual recomposition owing to bench expansion and increasing voluntary turnover has implications for the independence and autonomy of the judicial branch. David Mayhew describes how the activities and organization of Congress are tailored above all else to enhance the prospects for reelection.[47] If pushed to the extreme, the important task of "institutional maintenance" can be neglected. This in turn invites the possibility that Congress *as an institution* will be vulnerable to forays by the executive branch to aggrandize its power.

Part of this volume's significance is the parallel it suggests for the courts. The political behavior that has led to the constant recomposition of the bench[48] may have had the unintended consequence of compromising the role of the judiciary in the American political system, as the judiciary focuses more of its energy and attention on acculturation of new members than on routine maintenance and caseload matters. Will the consequence of redirecting the judiciary's attention from the business of the courts (decision making) weaken it vis-á-vis Congress and the executive? Additionally, a larger judiciary whose membership is continually changing could compromise the very concept of national law, being replaced instead by a "balkanization"[49] of the law around autonomous circuits.

Notes

Chapter 1

Epigraph from *Institutions, Institutional Change and Economic Performance* (Cambridge: Cambridge University Press, 1990), vii.

1. The tally includes the nine justices on the Supreme Court.

2. See Alfred H. Kelly and Winfred A. Harbison, *The American Constitution* (New York: W. W. Norton & Company, 1963), chaps. 17–18.

3. Kelly and Harbison, *The American Constitution,* 482.

4. See especially Fiorina's study of divided government, Morris Fiorina, *Divided Government* (New York: Macmillan, 1992). Other works on this question are discussed more fully later in the chapter. Unified government occurs when the president's party holds a majority of seats in both houses of Congress. Otherwise, government control is split or divided between the two major parties. One other nuance needs to be mentioned in the context of evaluating partisan transformation of the courts. It is important to consider periods of same-party control of the Senate even when the president's party does not govern the House of Representatives. This chamber, of course, commissions federal judges and so affects the rate of partisan appointments.

5. United States Judicial Conference, *Simple Fairness: The Case for Equitable Compensation of the Nation's Federal Judges* (Washington, D.C.: Government Printing Office, 1988). Indeed, retirements and resignations reached an all-time high in the past decade, averaging 4.3 percent annually, a level surpassing the 3.8 percent for the popularly elected Congress. See Deborah J. Barrow and Gary Zuk, "An Institutional Analysis of Turnover in the Lower Federal Courts, 1900–1987," *Journal of Politics* 52 (1990): 457–76.

6. There were 52 permanent (i.e., continuous) district court judgeships in 1868, the year before the advent of circuit judges. The figure including the latter court doubled by the turn of the century (1901), and did so again by 1937, at which point there were 209 members of the lower federal bench. The total reached 419 in 1966, and currently stands at 801.

7. On the idea of stability and the place of the judiciary in the separation of powers, see *The Federalist,* No. 80 and No. 81; more generally, see Alfred H. Kelly and Winfred A. Harbison, *The American Constitution* (New York: W. W. Norton & Company, 1963), especially chap. 5.

8. North, *Institutions, Institutional Change and Economic Performance,* 3.

9. Many scholars now refer to studies placing institutions at the center of their research designs as new institutionalism. The following studies are seminal among

those advancing this framework: Kenneth McNeil and James D. Thompson, "The Regeneration of Social Organizations," *American Sociological Review* 36 (1971): 624–37; James G. March and Johan P. Olsen, "The New Institutionalism: Organizational Factors in Political Life," *American Political Science Review* 78 (1984): 734–49; Rogers M. Smith, "Political Jurisprudence, The 'New Institutionalism,' and the Future of Public Law," *American Political Science Review* 82 (1988): 89–108; James G. March and Johan P. Olsen, *Rediscovering Institutions: The Organizational Basis of Politics* (New York: Free Press, 1989); Douglass C. North, *Institutions, Institutional Change and Economic Performance*; Douglass C. North, "Towards a Theory of Institutional Change," *Quarterly Review of Economics and Business* 31 (1991): 3–11; Douglass C. North, "Institutions and Economic Theory," *The American Economist* 36 (1992): 3–6; Susan R. Burgess, "Beyond Instrumental Politics: The New Institutionalism, Legal Rhetoric, & Judicial Supremacy," *Polity* 25 (1993): 445–59.

10. March and Olsen, *Rediscovering Institutions,* 16.

11. Illustrating with an example from the world of baseball, to execute a double play on a ground ball with a runner at first, the middle infielder need only tag second base (as opposed to tagging the runner) and then throw on to first to complete the play. The objective of the runner to second is to disrupt the infielder's throw to first while staying within the baselines so as not to be called out. To protect infielders from the onslaught of base runners, over time second-base umpires allowed the former simply to "be in the vicinity" of second rather than tagging it directly to record an out. Runners from first likewise were given latitude to stray from the baseline in their efforts to disrupt the play. The consequence of all of this is that on the double play both the size of second base and the width of the baseline have been enlarged with no change in the formal rules governing this play.

12. Walter F. Murphy explains the full range of these "political checks" and their effects on the politics of interinstitutional relationships in his celebrated works, *Congress and the Court* (Chicago: University of Chicago Press, 1962) and *Elements of Judicial Strategy* (Chicago: University of Chicago Press, 1964).

13. Some public-law scholars, however, have successfully employed institutional-level approaches in their studies. See, for example, Jeffrey A. Segal and Albert D. Cover, "Ideological Values and the Votes of U.S. Supreme Court Justices," *American Political Science Review* 83 (1989): 557–65; Lee Epstein, Thomas G. Walker, and William J. Dixon, "The Supreme Court and Criminal Justice Disputes: A Neo-Institutional Perspective," *American Journal of Political Science* 33 (1989): 825–41; Melinda Gann Hall and Paul Brace, "Neo-Institutionalism and Dissent in State Supreme Courts, *Journal of Politics* 52 (1990): 54–70; Gary Zuk, Gerard S. Gryski, and Deborah J. Barrow, "Partisan Transformation of the Federal Judiciary, 1869–1992," *American Politics Quarterly* 21 (1993): 439–57.

14. Though we are not offering a general survey of the literature on judicial decision making, a representative list would include: Sheldon Goldman, "Voting Behavior on the United States Courts of Appeals, 1961–1964," *American Political Science Review* 60 (1966): 374–83; S. Sidney Ulmer, "Social Background as an Indicator to the Votes of Supreme Court Justices in Criminal Cases: 1947–1956 Terms," *American Journal of Political Science* 17 (1973): 622–30; Sheldon Goldman, "Voting Behavior

on the U.S. Courts of Appeals Revisited," *American Political Science Review* 69 (1975): 491–506; J. Woodford Howard, "Role Perceptions and Behavior in Three U.S. Courts of Appeals," *Journal of Politics* 39 (1977): 916–38; C. Neal Tate, "Personal Attribute Models of the Voting Behavior of U.S. Supreme Court Justices: Liberalism in Civil Liberties and Economics Decisions, 1946–1978," *American Political Science Review* 75 (1981): 355–67; Robert A. Carp and C. K. Rowland, *Policymaking and Politics in the Federal District Courts* (Knoxville: University of Tennessee Press, 1983); James L. Gibson, "From Simplicity to Complexity: The Development of Theory in the Study of Judicial Behavior," *Political Behavior* 7 (1983): 7–49.

15. In a series of studies revising the basis of partisan transformations in electoral realignment theory, Carmines and Stimson provide a rigorous analysis of the causal dynamics of evolutionary processes. Though the elements of our study are different, we benefit substantially from their discussion of change and causality over time. See especially Edward G. Carmines and James A. Stimson, "Issue Evolution, Population Replacement, and Normal Partisan Change," *American Political Science Review* 75 (1981): 107–18; Edward G. Carmines and James A. Stimson, "On the Structure and Sequence of Issue Evolution," *American Political Science Review* 80 (1986): 901–20; Edward G. Carmines and James A. Stimson, *Issue Evolution: Race and the Transformation of American Politics* (Princeton, N.J.: Princeton University Press, 1989). Also, for another insightful treatment that is especially relevant to the diachronic study of institutions, see Joseph Cooper and David W. Brady, "Toward a Diachronic Analysis of Congress," *American Political Science Review* 75 (1981): 988–1006; and the continuation of the dialogue by Samuel C. Patterson, "Understanding Congress in the Long Run: A Comment on Joseph Cooper and David W. Brady, 'Toward a Diachronic Theory of Congress,'" *American Political Science Review* 75 (1981): 1007–9; and Nelson W. Polsby, "Studying Congress through Time: A Comment on Joseph Cooper and David Brady, 'Toward a Diachronic Analysis of Congress,'" *American Political Science Review* 75 (1981): 1010–12.

16. For analytical and historical treatments of the impact that interinstitutional struggles have had on the U.S. Supreme Court and the lower federal courts, see Murphy, *Congress and the Court* and *Elements of Judicial Strategy*; Peter G. Fish, *The Politics of Federal Judicial Administration* (Princeton, N.J.: Princeton University Press, 1973); and Gregory A. Caldeira, "Public Opinion and the U.S. Supreme Court," *American Political Science Review* 81 (1987): 1139–53.

17. This has been asserted at least as long ago as 1885 and as recently as 1994. See Woodrow Wilson, *Congressional Government* (Boston: Houghton, Mifflin and Company, 1885), especially chap. 5; Richard E. Cohen, *Changing Course in Washington* (New York: Macmillan Publishing Company, 1994). More generally, see, for example, James MacGregor Burns, *The Deadlock of Democracy* (Englewood Cliffs, N.J.: Prentice-Hall, 1967); James Sundquist, *Constitutional Reform and Effective Government* (Washington, D.C.: Brookings Institution, 1986); and Sundquist, "Needed: A Political Theory for the New Era of Coalition Government in the United States," *Political Science Quarterly* 103 (1988): 613–35.

18. David R. Mayhew, *Divided We Govern: Party Control, Lawmaking, and Investigations, 1946–1990* (New Haven, Conn.: Yale University Press, 1991).

19. Roger H. Davidson, "The Presidency and Three Eras of the Modern Congress," in James A. Thurber, ed., *Divided Democracy* (Washington, D.C.: Congressional Quarterly Press, 1991). See also Mark P. Petracca, "Divided Government and the Risks of Constitutional Reform," *PS: Political Science & Politics* 24 (1991): 634–37; Fiorina, *Divided Government.*

20. Sean Q Kelly, "Divided We Govern? A Reassessment," *Polity* 25 (1993): 475–84. See also David R. Mayhew, "Reply: Let's Stick With the Longer List," *Polity* 25 (1993): 485–88; Kelly, "Response: Let's Stick With the Larger Questions," *Polity* 25 (1993): 489–90.

21. David W. Rohde and Dennis M. Simon, "Presidential Vetoes and Congressional Response: A Study of Institutional Conflict," *American Journal of Political Science* 29 (1985): 397–427.

22. Lilliard E. Richardson, Jr. and John M. Scheb, II, "Divided Government and the Supreme Court," *American Politics Quarterly* 21 (1993): 458–72.

23. Lloyd Cutler, "Now Is the Time for All Good Men," *William and Mary Law Review* 30 (1989): 387–402; David Brady and Morris Fiorina, "The Ruptured Legacy: Presidential-Congressional Relations in Historical Perspective," in Larry Berman, ed., *Looking Back on the Reagan Presidency* (Baltimore: Johns Hopkins University Press, 1990), 270–76; Mathew McCubbins, "Party Governance and U.S. Budget Deficits: Divided Government and Fiscal Stalemate," in Alberto Alesina and Geoffrey Carliner, eds., *Politics and Economics in the 1980s* (Chicago: University of Chicago Press, 1991), 83–111; Mathew D. McCubbins, "Government on Lay-Away: Federal Spending and Deficits under Divided Party Control," in Gary W. Cox and Samuel Kernell, eds., *The Politics of Divided Government* (Boulder, Colo.: Westview Press, 1991), 113–53; Gary W. Cox and Mathew D. McCubbins, "Divided Control of Fiscal Policy," in Cox and Kernell, *Politics of Divided Government,* 155–75; Donald F. Kettl, *Deficit Politics* (New York: Macmillan, 1992); and James Cox, Gregory Hager, and David Lowery, "Regime Change in Presidential and Congressional Budgeting: Role Discontinuity or Role Evolution," *American Journal of Political Science* 37 (1993): 88–118.

24. Fiorina, *Divided Government,* see especially chap. 6.

25. Parenthetically, in reviewing the consequences of divided government for nominations to the Supreme Court, Fiorina observes: "There is a much larger category of federal district and circuit court judges, but I have been unable to locate tallies of nominations and their fates." Fiorina, *Divided Government,* 97.

26. See James D. Thompson, *Organizations in Action* (New York: McGraw-Hill, 1967); Francis E. Rourke, *Bureaucracy, Politics, and Public Policy* (Boston: Little, Brown, 1969); and Gerard S. Gryski, *Bureaucratic Policy Making in a Technological Society* (Cambridge, Mass.: Schenkman Publishing Company, 1981).

27. Congress also has the authority to create temporary judgeships by stipulating a discontinuance of authority and funding for the position, either once the person occupying the judgeship vacates the position or after the next vacancy in a judgeship on the court. Historically, the tendency is to authorize temporary positions when there is no clear indication that an increase in caseload within a particular jurisdiction will be a

permanent one. The creation of such judgeships under these circumstances is sporadic and infrequent since the 1960s. In several cases Congress used temporary judgeships as means to resolve administrative matters that raised political questions. The most prominent examples were the conversion of the old Commerce Court positions to temporary appellate judgeships upon the abolition of that court in 1913 and the creation of four temporary positions for the Fifth Circuit Court of Appeals to bypass the political gridlock over dividing that court into two circuits. See Erwin C. Surrency, *History of the Federal Courts* (New York: Oceana Publications, 1987); and Deborah J. Barrow and Thomas G. Walker, *A Court Divided: The Politics of Judicial Reform and the Fifth Circuit Court of Appeals* (New Haven, Conn.: Yale University Press, 1988). Regardless of the reason for their creation, however, only rarely has Congress not converted a temporary position into a permanent one.

28. There are three notable instances in which the size of the lower bench decreased from its chartering under the Federal Judiciary Act of 1789 through 1992. All occurred during periods of political transformation in this country. The legislation passed by the outgoing Federalist Party, for example, creating 19 circuit judgeships under the Acts of February 13 and February 27, 1801 was remanded except for the three positions on the Supreme Court of the District of Columbia by the Jeffersonians (Act of March 8, 1802). This latter court stayed in operation until 1863, when it too was abolished (Act of March 3, 1863) during the general federal court upheaval and reorganization of the Civil War. Several years later, the Western District of Louisiana received the same fate (Act of July 27, 1866). Finally, the U.S. Commerce Court created during Taft's presidency (Act of June 18, 1910) was legislated out of existence by the Democrats under the Act of October 22, 1913. Four of the five judges appointed to this court retained their commissions on the courts of appeals, however. No successors to their positions were allowed.

29. See McNeil and Thompson, "The Regeneration of Social Organizations."

30. U.S. Judiciary, Judicial Conference, *Simple Fairness: The Case for Equitable Compensation of the Nation's Federal Judges,* submitted to the 1988 Commission on Executive, Legislative, and Judicial Salaries.

31. See especially Lawrence C. Dodd and Richard L. Schott, *Congress and the Administrative State* (New York: John Wiley and Sons, 1979); John R. Hibbing, "Voluntary Retirements from the House in the Twentieth Century," *Journal of Politics* 44 (1982): 1020–34; John R. Hibbing, "Voluntary Retirements from the U.S. House of Representatives: Who Quits?," *American Journal of Political Science* 26 (1982): 467–84; John R. Hibbing, *Congressional Careers: Contours of Life in the U.S. House of Representatives* (Chapel Hill: University of North Carolina Press, 1991); and Paul Brace, "A Probabilistic Approach to Retirement from the U.S. Congress," *Legislative Studies Quarterly* 10 (1985): 107–23.

32. This lesson was not lost on recent presidents. Both of George Bush's nominees to the High Court came from the courts of appeals, as did five of the six made by Ronald Reagan (counting the elevation of Rehnquist to chief justice and the failed Bork and Ginsburg nominations), Ford's lone appointment, and four of the six Nixon nominees (including the unsuccessful nominations of Haynsworth and Carswell).

Jimmy Carter, who made the largest number of appointments to new positions of any president in history, made none to the U.S. Supreme Court, something that had not happened since the presidency of Andrew Johnson.

Chapter 2

The first epigraph is from *Journal of the American Judicature Society* 22 (1938), 151 and 152. In the second epigraph, Walter's remarks refer to the 1954 omnibus judgeship bill and why there was a backlog of cases in Pennsylvania. *Congressional Record,* July 30, 1953, 10595.

1. The outgoing Federalists authorized 19 circuit judgeships in 1801, 3 of which went unfilled until Jefferson's first term. The commissions of all but the District of Columbia circuit court judges were remanded by the Seventh Congress, which was controlled by Jefferson's Democratic-Republican Party. This court stayed in operation until 1863, when it too was abolished. See *Federal Cases,* Vols. 1 and 30 (Minneapolis: West Publishing Co.), U.S. Senate, Committee on the Judiciary, and U.S. Judiciary, Judicial Conference of the United States, *Judges of the United States,* 1983 for a complete listing and short biographical sketch of all of the judges on the circuit courts from 1801–63. A brief overview of the circuit court of the District of Columbia is in U.S. Judiciary, Judicial Conference, Bicentennial Committee, *History of the United States Court of Appeals for the District of Columbia Circuit in the Country's Bicentennial Year,* 1976, and Theodore Voorhees, "The District of Columbia Courts: A Judicial Anomaly," *Catholic University Law Review* 29 (1980): 917–37. The Act of April 10, 1869, authorized the appointment of 9 circuit judges to reduce the circuit-level workload of justices on the U.S. Supreme Court (see chap. 3). Their numbers grew to 20 with the passage of the Act of March 3, 1891, which established the U.S. Courts of Appeals.

2. See Evan A. Evans, "Political Influence in the Selection of Federal Judges," *Wisconsin Law Review* (1948): 330–51; Rita W. Cooley, "Judicial Appointments in the Eisenhower Administration (January 1952–June 1958)," *Social Science* 34 (1959): 10–14; U.S. Senate, Committee on the Judiciary, *Legislative History of the Courts of Appeals,* 92d Congress, 1972; Kermit L. Hall, *The Politics of Justice: Lower Federal Judicial Selection and the Second Party System, 1829–61* (Lincoln: University of Nebraska Press, 1979); *Judges of the United States;* Sheldon Goldman, "Characteristics of Eisenhower and Kennedy Appointees to the Lower Federal Courts," *Western Political Quarterly* 28 (1965): 755–62; Sheldon Goldman, "Bush's Judicial Legacy: The Final Imprint," *Judicature* 76 (1993): 282–97; and Henry J. Abraham, *Justices and Presidents: A Political History of Appointments to the Supreme Court* (New York: Oxford University Press, 1974).

3. See Jon R. Bond, "The Politics of Court Structure: The Addition of New Federal Judges, 1949–1978," *Law and Politics Quarterly* 2 (1980): 181–88; Gary Zuk, Gerard S. Gryski, and Deborah J. Barrow, "Partisan Transformation of the Federal Judiciary, 1869–1992," *American Politics Quarterly* 2 (1993): 439–57.

4. See Peter G. Fish, *The Politics of Federal Judicial Administration* (Princeton, N.J.: Princeton University Press, 1973), 3–90.

5. Whereas the Conference routinely bundled its judgeship requests in its annual submission to Congress, not until 1935 would omnibus measures become the accepted vehicle of bench expansion on Capitol Hill.

6. The percentages are based on the number of permanent positions authorized by the Judicial Code of 1922, through the most recent judgeship bill legislated in 1990.

7. See Charles A. Johnson and Ricky Rosenblum, "Retirements by Federal Judges: Exploring the Issue of Political Timing," presented at the Annual Meeting of the Midwest Political Science Association, Chicago, April 1987; Deborah J. Barrow and Gary Zuk, "An Institutional Analysis of Turnover in the Lower Federal Courts," *Journal of Politics* 52 (1990): 457–76.

8. If this were not the case then any tendencies observed would be skewed toward the district courts, whose numbers outstrip those of the courts of appeals.

9. Analysis of the two lower federal courts as one entity is appropriate in this context because the major elements of institutional change we explore are virtually the same for the two courts from 1869–1992. The partisan appointment rate on the district courts, for instance, averaged 93.5 percent compared to 92.2 percent on the courts of appeals. Appointments to new positions as a proportion of all judicial appointments averaged 32.2 percent on the district courts and only 2 percentage points lower on the appellate bench. The mean partisan voluntary turnover rate was 54.1 percent for the district courts and 52.6 percent for the circuit courts. Indeed, there is very little difference in age at time of appointment (50 versus 53) and at time of resignation (56 and 59) or retirement (70 and 71), and so length of service on the two courts is about the same as well.

10. Unless otherwise indicated, the data are based on the number of sitting judges rather than authorized positions. The appropriate unit of time for bench expansion is a congress rather than a year. Appointees nominated in the first year of a congress frequently have their confirmation proceedings carried into the second, but if action is not completed by the close of the congress then the nomination fails by default and a new one must be made in the succeeding session. George Bush fell victim to this cycle by sending names up to the Senate at a rather deliberate pace. During the 1992 presidential election year, the Democratically controlled Senate failed to complete action on scores of nominations, thereby furnishing their standard bearer, Bill Clinton, with over 100 vacancies to fill, a record number. See Stephen Labaton, "Clinton Expected to Change Makeup of Federal Courts," *New York Times,* March 8, 1993, A1 and A9.

11. Judges on the Supreme (later District) Court of the District of Columbia and the Courts of Appeals of the District of Columbia, like their colleagues on the High Court, were on occasion promoted from associate to chief judge. The elevation created a vacancy and so an executive appointment opportunity. The practice ended in the 1950s when the position of chief judge became based on seniority.

12. Information is also available on both confirmed and unconfirmed recess appointments.

13. A numbering system for seats on the U.S. Supreme Court has been in use for quite some time now, so positional histories as well as the characteristics of the justices occupying particular seats can be studied. We know of no parallel efforts for the lower federal bench until the present one.

14. We have similar data on the 52 judges who were on the bench when Grant assumed office in 1869 (see chap. 3).

15. The difference between the aggregate appointment and leaving figures is the 693 judges in active service at the close of the Bush administration. While the number of authorized positions is over 800, there were over 100 vacancies when the 102d Congress adjourned, owing either to the reluctance of the Senate to act on a slew of nominees in a presidential election year or to a score of judges who left in the wake of the 1992 election.

16. Rather than being aggregated by year, the horizontal axis denotes the percentage of Republican judges on the bench when each president left office. Since the tenure of various presidents differs, this results in some minor distortion in the presentation, but the metric used allows all but Garfield's administration—which is combined with Arthur's—to be profiled.

17. Broken down by subperiod, the figures are remarkably consistent: 73.9 percent Republicans in the first, 74.2 percent Democrats in the second, and 72.6 percent Republicans in the third.

18. The only interlevel deviation is an 88.4 percent same-party rate for the courts of appeals in the first subperiod. Since then the percentages are 93.5 percent in the middle era and 93.4 percent in the contemporary period. The partisan appointment rate on the district courts ranged from 91.9 to 95.1 percent.

19. The classic treatment of the subject is Richard E. Neustadt, *Presidential Power* (New York: John Wiley & Sons, 1960).

20. Evan A. Evans, "Political Influences in the Selection of Federal Judges." Evans served on the Seventh Circuit Court of Appeals from 1916 to 1948.

21. The figure for the judiciary includes vacancies; counting only sitting judges the judiciary is currently 136 percent larger than Congress.

22. Bench growth on the district courts outpaced that on the courts of appeals during the second and third eras, periods that coincide with the major increases in new positions from omnibus judgeship legislation. Indeed in all such cases but one (the Act of June 18, 1968), the lion's share of additional judgeships were created for district courts. The higher rate for the circuit courts from 1869–1932 is a historical artifact: the number of judges on these courts rose from zero in 1868 to 45 by 1933 (see chap. 3). The 1968 act authorized additional positions only on the courts of appeals in an effort to stagger bench expansion by level of court. The complement of new district court seats was legislated by the Act of June 2, 1970. The bill for the Carter administration returned to the traditional format of creating new judgeships for both courts.

23. Since FDR's administration when omnibus judgeship legislation became the vehicle for bench expansion, the cross-party appointment rate for replacement positions is 6.9 percent, and 7.3 percent for new seats.

24. Resignees from the courts of appeals, not surprisingly, are three to four years older than the cohort on the district courts. In Table 2.2 we do not report the data by party of the judge because the differences in the calculations by party of the president are inconsequential.

25. Twenty-one percent of the voluntary leavers from 1869–1932 resigned, and 15.9 percent retired. The percentages for both groups were somewhat higher (23.5 percent and 20.4 percent, respectively) on the courts of appeals.

26. The compression in salaries during the 1980s raises the question of whether judges are increasingly forsaking the bench for material reasons. In this respect, we note that resigners as a percentage of all leavers rose slightly from the second to the third subperiods, albeit only by one percentage point.

27. Regarding interlevel differences by subperiod, appeals court retirees left with fewer years of service than their colleagues on the district courts, which is to be expected given that almost half were elevated and so they had already logged some time on the district bench (the average length of district court service prior to elevation is 8 years). Nevertheless, the gap between the two plummeted from 8 years in the first era to two in the second, and only one year in the third. With the age at retirement on the two courts being about the same from 1869–1992, and only two year's difference in length of service, the retirement patterns of district and appellate court judges now are virtually the same.

28. Actually the retirement figures, large as they are, understate the case, particularly on the courts of appeals. This is because in calculating voluntary leaving, the denominator of the construct (all departures) appropriately includes elevations (which create vacancies), but judges vacating their positions in this way are changing offices rather than leaving the system. This nuance pertains especially to the district bench, the source of almost half of all circuit court appointments, whereas only a fraction (3.6 percent) of all appellate judges go on to serve on the High Court. Omitting elevations, the overall proportion leaving through retirement stands at 83.3 percent: 83.2 percent on the district courts, and 83.5 percent on the courts of appeals.

29. Sixty-six percent of all who resigned their judicial commissions and 68.6 percent of those who filled vacancies occurring through elevations did so during a Republican administration. The figures vary by subperiod but not by level of court, ebbing during the 1933–68 era of Democratic party control and peaking during the two eras of Republican dominance of the Oval Office.

30. Historically the percentages are slightly higher for district judges (54.1 to 52.8 percent).

31. Among the 23 administrations under study, the same-party leaving rates during the Kennedy, Carter, and Johnson presidencies were the fifth, sixth, and ninth highest, respectively.

32. In documenting same-party leaving behavior, we are under no illusion that all judges try to time for political reasons their departures from the bench. We are trying to discern whether or not there is a pattern. The point is that, especially in the contemporary era, retirement is the modal path off the bench. Given the increasingly large number of judges choosing this option, even if political timing in retiring occurs only marginally, a president will be provided with a substantially larger number of appointment opportunities than would be the case otherwise.

33. Perhaps not coincidentally, the highest partisan turnover rates (100 percent) came during the Hayes, Garfield, and Arthur presidencies, all of which, of course, immediately preceded the Cleveland presidency, and thus in staffing the federal courts benefited from a prolonged period of Republican rule.

34. The percentages by subperiod are 48.9 percent, 39.7 percent, and 43.4 percent.

35. Eleven presidents elevated 50 percent or more of their appointees. All are Republicans.

36. Carter's presidency is the exception. At the start of his term in office, Democrats occupied nearly half of the lower federal bench, comprising even higher percentages on the district courts (see chap. 5). Yet Carter's elevation rate was the fourth lowest in the span of the data. The reason for the incongruity is the extraordinarily large number of women, African American, and Latino jurists commissioned by the 39th president who were largely selected from outside the confines of the district courts.

37. The irony with Nixon's inability to take partisan control of the lower courts stands in marked contrast to his political realignment of the Supreme Court. See James F. Simon, *In His Own Image: The Supreme Court in Richard Nixon's America* (New York: David McKay, 1973).

38. The appointees of Hayes, Garfield/Arthur, Cleveland (both terms), Ford, and Bush represented less than 30 percent of the bench at the close of their administrations.

39. The three administrations having the largest presidential cohorts are those of Grant and the two Roosevelts.

40. U.S. Judicial Conference, 1978, 1983.

41. 1st series (March 1880–Nov. 1924), 2d series (Nov. 1924/Jan. 1925–92), St. Paul, Minn.: West Publishing Company.

42. 1894–97 (see especially vols. 1 and 30), St. Paul, Minn.: West Publishing Company.

43. U.S. Senate, 1828–present.

44. U.S. Senate, Committee on the Judiciary, 1972.

45. U.S. Senate, Committee on the Judiciary, 1977–80.

46. U.S. Congress, Congressional Research Service, *Nomination and Confirmation Actions: 97th Congress,* 97th Congress, 1981–82; *Nomination and Confirmation Actions: 98th Congress,* 98th Congress, 1983–84; *Judicial Nominations by President Reagan during the 99th Congress,* 99th Congress, 1985–86; *President Reagan's Judicial Nominations during the 100th Congress: A Statistical Overview and Listing of Nominees and Dates of Confirmation or Other Final Action,* 100th Congress, 1988; *President Bush's Judicial Nominations during the 101st Congress: A Statistical Overview and Listing of Nominees and Dates of Confirmation or Other Final Action,* 101st Congress, 1990; *President Bush's Judicial Nominations during the 102nd Congress: A Statistical Overview and Listing of Nominees and Dates of Confirmation or Other Final Action,* 102d Congress, 1992.

47. Harold W. Chase, Samuel Krislov, Keith O. Boyum, and Jerry N. Clark, *Biographical Dictionary of the Federal Judiciary* (Detroit: Gale Research Company, 1976).

48. U.S. Judiciary, Federal Judicial Center (1969–89); Administrative Office of the United States Courts (1990–present).

49. *Biographical Dictionary of the Federal Judiciary.*

50. U.S. Department of Justice, *Register of the Department of Justice and the Courts of the United States,* 1870–present.

51. U.S. Senate, *Journal of the Executive Proceedings of the Senate of the United States of America,* 1828–present.

52. U.S. Senate, Committee on the Judiciary, *Legislative History of the United*

States Courts of Appeals and the Judges Who Served During the Period 1801 Through May 1972, 92d Congress, 1972.

53. Edwin Surrency, "The Federal District Court Judges and the History of Their Courts," *Federal Rules Decisions* 103 (1967): 139–310.

54. Mary Reincke, ed., *The American Bench: Judges of the Nation* (Minneapolis: Reginald Bishop Forster and Associates, 1977); Nancy Lichterman, ed., *The American Bench: Judges of the Nation* (Minneapolis: Reginald Bishop Forster and Associates, 1979); Sarah Livermore, ed., *The American Bench: Judges of the Nation* (Sacramento: Reginald Bishop Forster and Associates, Inc., 1985–86); Marie T. Hough, ed., *The American Bench: Judges of the Nation* (Sacramento: Reginald Bishop Forster and Associates, Inc., 1987–88); Marie T. Hough, ed., *The American Bench: Judges of the Nation* (Sacramento: Forster-Long, Inc., 1989–90).

55. Stuart W. Dornette and Robert P. Cross, eds., *Federal Judiciary Almanac* (New York: John Wiley, 1984, 1986).

56. Charles B. Brownson and Anna L. Brownson, eds., *Judicial Staff Directory* (Mt. Vernon, Va.: Congressional Staff Directory, Ltd., 1987, 1988, 1989 [Anna Brownson only]).

57. *Almanac of the Federal Judiciary* (Englewood Cliffs: Prentice-Hall, 1984–89).

58. *Who's Who in America* (Chicago: Marquis Who's Who, Inc., various volumes); *Who Was Who in America* (Chicago: Marquis Who's Who, Inc., various volumes); *Who's Who in American Law* (Chicago: Marquis Who's Who, Inc., various volumes); *Who's Who in American Politics* (New York: Bowker, various issues).

59. Allen Johnson, *Dictionary of American Biography* (New York: Charles Scribner's Sons, 1928–58).

60. *The National Cyclopedia of American Biography* (New York: James T. White & Co., 1891–present).

61. Robert Sobel, *Biographical Directory of the United States Executive Branch, 1774–1977,* 3d ed. (Westport, Conn.: Greenwood Press, 1977).

62. U.S. Congress, *Biographical Directory of the United States Congress, 1774–1989,* 101st Congress, 1989.

Chapter 3

Epigraph from *Congressional Record,* December 10, 1921, 201.

1. Congressional Quarterly, *Guide To Congress,* 4th ed. (Washington: Congressional Quarterly Press, 1993), 93–94. Democrats enjoyed unified control on only four occasions (53d, 63d–65th); 11 times government was divided (see note 38).

2. See Kathryn Turner, "The Midnight Judges," *University of Pennsylvania Law Review* 109 (1960/61): 494–523 for a detailing of the circumstances surrounding the creation of these ill-fated courts, along with brief profiles of most of the judges.

3. Information on the names of these judges, their judicial offices, appointing president, date, and the reason for the commission came from U.S. Senate, *Journal of the Executive Proceedings of the Senate of the United States,* vols. 1–16 (1828–61); *Federal Cases,* vols. 1 and 30; Edwin Surrency, "Federal District Court Judges and the History of Their Courts," *Federal Rules Decisions* 103 (1967): 139–310; U.S. Judi-

ciary, Judicial Conference, *Judges of the United States,* 1978, 1983. See Kermit L. Hall, *The Politics of Justice: Lower Federal Judicial Selection and the Second Party System, 1829–61* (Lincoln: University of Nebraska Press, 1979), for an analysis of the politics of judicial selection from the John Quincy Adams through the James Buchanan administrations. Evan A. Evans, a former federal judge, surveyed lower federal court appointments from Grover Cleveland's first term through Franklin D. Roosevelt's second term in "Political Influences in the Selection of Federal Judges," *Wisconsin Law Review* (1948): 330–51.

4. The positions on the California and District of Columbia Circuits were abolished in 1863. The Supreme Court of the District of Columbia (later called the D.C. District Court), comprised of four Article III district court judges, was created in that same year. Further restructuring took place in 1866 when the Western District Court of Louisiana and a provisional judgeship for the state were abolished, leaving one federal judge for the entire state.

5. The number is over 200 if temporary positions such as the 5 circuit court judgeships created by the Act of June 18, 1910, or the 23 on the district courts (Act of September 22, 1922) are included. Most of these temporary lines were converted to permanent status by the omnibus judgeship acts of 1935 and 1938.

6. The figures are based on the first U.S. Judicial Code, detailing dates of the structuring and staffing of the lower federal courts from the Federal Judiciary Act of 1789 to 1911 (Act of March 3), and a subsequent codification under Title 28 (1940) listing additional judgeships from 1911 to 1940.

7. The one exception came during the administration of John Tyler. Elected to the vice presidency on the Whig ticket and succeeding William Henry Harrison to the presidency following the latter's death in office, Tyler nominated more Democrats than Whigs to federal judgeships according to the figures in Hall, *The Politics of Justice,* 189. A former Democrat himself, Tyler tried to use patronage to curry favor with the party and win its nomination for president, an effort that failed, of course.

8. There were also four U.S. territorial courts (Alaska, Canal Zone, Hawaii, Puerto Rico) in operation by 1932. Eight term judges were employed on these courts.

9. New districts were created in Nebraska (1867), Colorado (1876), Montana (1889), North Dakota (1890), South Dakota (1890), Washington (1890), Idaho (1890), Wyoming (1890), Utah (1894), Arizona (1913), and New Mexico (1910). Two judicial districts were authorized for Oklahoma (1906), and a second was added for Washington (1905). Following the court reorganization of 1929 the new district courts were distributed over the Eighth through Tenth Circuits.

10. Caseload statistics were derived from the U.S. Department of Justice, *Annual Report of the Attorney General of the United States,* various years, and Richard A. Posner, *The Federal Courts: Crisis and Reform* (Cambridge: Harvard University Press, 1985), 350–51. Zuk, Gryski, and Barrow ("Partisan Transformation of the Federal Courts") analyze the effect of caseload on new positions and turnover on the lower federal courts. The study finds that in each instance caseload had a significant but modest impact that was overshadowed by political variables—such as whether government was politically unified or divided—in accounting for new positions, and the party of the sitting president, in evaluating departures.

11. 16 Stat. 44.

12. U.S. Judiciary, Judicial Conference, Bicentennial Committee, *A History of the United States Court of Appeals for the Eighth Circuit,* 1976, 13.

13. Peter G. Fish, *The Politics of Judicial Administration* (Princeton, N.J.: Princeton University Press, 1973), 77.

14. Only 18 of the 86 judicial districts in existence in 1932 did not receive additional positions from 1869–1932. Ten were located in former states of the Confederacy.

15. 42 Stat. 839. Students of the judiciary sometimes list the judgeship bills of 1927 and 1929 as omnibus acts. These bills, however, while often introduced on the same day (e.g., March 3, 1927), legislated additional positions either for individual districts or districts within the same state on a case-by-case basis rather than as a package. Strictly speaking, then, the second omnibus judgeship bill was not passed until 1935.

16. Four presidents (J. Q. Adams, Van Buren, William H. Harrison, and Tyler) were given no new judicial positions by the Congress in the years prior to the advent of omnibus judgeships. Two (Taylor and Johnson) were given one position, and five (Adams, Jefferson, Jackson, Fillmore, and Buchanan) received two additional judgeships. Madison was given three positions, Polk and Pierce five, Monroe six, Lincoln nine, and Washington seventeen.

17. Fish, *The Politics of Judicial Administration,* 14–39.

18. Henry F. Pringle, *The Life and Times of William Howard Taft,* 2 vols. (New York: Farrar & Rinehart, 1939), 992–1006.

19. Remarks of Rep. Bertrand H. Snell (R–NY), discussing the report of the attorney general, *Congressional Record,* December 9, 1921, 146.

20. Letter of Attorney General H. M. Daugherty to House Judiciary Chair Joseph Walsh (R–MA), published in the *Congressional Record,* December 9, 1921, 150.

21. An assortment of other issues were contained in the bill, or at least proposed. As mentioned below, in all but one instance (MD-TN) the district judgeships ultimately authorized were for temporary positions. A Senate Judiciary Committee amendment provided that at any time after four years following the enactment of the bill, when a vacancy occurred in any district receiving one of the temporary positions, the attorney general, in concert with the senior circuit judge, would certify whether the vacancy should go unfilled (i.e., abolish the position) or be converted to a permanent office. This proposal created quite a stir, and not just from the minority, over the argument that this procedure violated the Article III power of Congress, who alone had authority to create new positions. In the final version of the bill, that power was left solely to Congress. Another proposal to alleviate caseload was the creation of "misdemeanor courts," to be presided over by Article I rather than Article III judges, but the idea obviously did not find its way into the final bill.

22. Remarks of Sen. Albert B. Cummins (R–IA), *Congressional Record,* March 31, 1922, 4854.

23. Article III, Section 1. Some also felt that the judiciary would tread on the executive power of the attorney general, one of whose responsibilities was to report to Congress on the state of the courts.

24. Remarks of Sen. John K. Shields (D–TN), *Congressional Record,* March 31, 1922, 4855.

25. Remarks of Rep. Clarence F. Lea (D–CA), *Congressional Record,* December 10, 1921, 202.

26. The most bitterly contested feature of the bill, nonetheless, was Section 5, which amended Section 14 of the Judicial Code. It provided that "to expedite the business or relieve the accumulation or urgency of business in any district court" the Chief Justice may, when certified to him by the senior judge of a judicial circuit, temporarily transfer one or more district judges from outside the circuit. In point of fact, for some time judges from the First Circuit had been assigned temporarily to the Second, primarily to alleviate the workload in the Southern District of New York. That practice invited no controversy, nor did Section 4 of the bill that granted senior circuit judges the authority to transfer temporarily judges from district to district in the same circuit. The charge was led primarily by southern Democrats such as Rep. William F. Stevenson (D–SC), who feared the onslaught of a second wave of carpetbaggers:

> We used to have a satrap from Baltimore who went down there [South Carolina] and put many of our people in jail, and they had to be delivered from jail by the Supreme Court of the United States, and some of them had to suffer until they were delivered by the pardon of President Grant, although the statute under which they were put in jail was subsequently practically declared to be null and void and without authority of the Constitution.

Southerners were concerned that the creation of "a perambulatory light dragoon flying skirmish-drill squadron":

> . . . and this power to assign judges carries with it the power to select a judge with known preconceived opinions to acquit or convict defendants and to decide civil cases in a certain way. The opportunities for abuse and oppression are apparent, broad, and indisputable.

Authorization to create a cadre of roving judges did not find its way into the final version of the bill. The respective cites for the above three quotes are *Congressional Record,* December 10, 1921, 204; Remarks of Sen. John S. Williams (D–MS), *Congressional Record,* April 6, 1922, 5107; remarks of Sen. John K. Shields (D–TN), *Congressional Record,* March 31, 1922, 4860.

27. *Congressional Record,* December 9, 1921, 166.

28. Remarks of Thomas U. Sisson (D–MS), *Congressional Record,* December 9, 1921, 164.

29. Remarks of Rep. Andrew Jackson Montague (D–VA), *Congressional Record,* December 9, 1921, 157.

30. Landis resigned his judicial commission in 1923.

31. Remarks of Sen. Lee S. Overman (D–NC), *Congressional Record,* April 6, 1922, 5096.

32. *Congressional Record,* December 21, 1921, 209. In addition to numerous changes in the Judicial Code, the bill provided for two new positions in Massachusetts and the Southern District of New York, and one each in the Eastern District of New

York, Eastern and Western Districts of Pennsylvania, Northern District of Texas, Southern District of Florida, Eastern District of Michigan, Northern District of Ohio, Middle District of Tennessee, Northern and Eastern Districts of Illinois, Minnesota, Eastern and Western Districts of Missouri, Eastern District of Oklahoma, Montana, Arizona, and the Northern and Southern Districts of California. All of the new judgeships except in the Middle District of Tennessee allowed no successors. The Act of August 19, 1935 converted many of these temporary lines into permanent ones.

33. *Congressional Record,* April 7, 1922, 5174. The Senate added positions in New Mexico and New Jersey, and an additional judgeship for the Fourth Circuit.

34. Federal judges saw their salary substantially increased, along with their numbers, to make service more rewarding. A district judge in 1869, for instance, was paid between $3,500 and $5,000 annually. Salaries gradually rose to $7,500 in the interlude before the inception of the Federal Judicial Conference in 1922. Four years later the figure was $10,000. Salaries for appeals court judges, by comparison, climbed from $8,500 in 1925 to $12,500 the following year. See Richard A. Posner, *The Federal Courts: Crisis and Reform* (Cambridge, Mass.: Harvard University Press, 1985), 347–48.

35. Congress created 47 new and permanent judgeships on the lower federal courts between 1922 and 1932, 36 percent of the total increase from 1869–1932. The number is 70 if temporary positions are included.

36. See Fish, *The Politics of Judicial Administration,* 66. Taft exercised considerable influence in appointments to the High Court as well. See Walter F. Murphy, "In His Own Image: Mr. Chief Justice Taft and Supreme Court Appointment," in *The Supreme Court Review* (Chicago: University of Chicago Press, 1961), 159–93, for a classic study of the role played by the Chief Justice in appointments to the Taft Court. Taft's influence was strengthened enormously by the unique qualities he brought to the position of Chief Justice as president emeritus of a reinvigorated Republican Party. See also Murphy, 190–91.

37. The total includes the five appointees under the Act of June 18, 1910 to the U.S. Commerce Court who also were assigned to the circuit courts. The Commerce Court was subsequently abolished by the 63d Congress (Act of October 22, 1913), governed by the Democrats. All of the judges except Robert Archbald, who was removed from office, retained their commissions on the courts of appeals, however.

38. Eleven of the 32 congresses from 1869 to 1932 were not controlled by the president's party: 44th and 45th (House); 46th (House and Senate); 48th (House); 49th and 50th (Senate); 52d (House); 54th (House and Senate); 62d (House); 66th (House and Senate); 72d (House).

39. 16 Stat. 45.

40. The Act of February 25, 1919, legislated during the 65th Congress governed by the Democrats, clarified previous retirement legislation. The 1869 measure, for example, entitled judges who resigned at age 70 with 10 years of continuous service to receive for the remainder of their lives the same salary paid in their last year of service. The Act of February 15, 1909 changed the anniversary salary date from the last year of a decade of continuous service to the first year. The act of March 3, 1911, establishing the Judicial Code of the United States, restored the language of the 1869 act. The 1919

act reaffirmed the conditions of "resignation" with pay. The 1919 act also established senior service on a completely voluntary basis. This was referred to as "retiring," as opposed to resigning with full salary. The act included a controversial section that, in effect, pressured senior members of the bench to step down. If a judge eligible to "resign" elected instead to remain in office yet was deemed by the president unable to carry out fully the duties of a federal judge by reason of permanent mental or physical disability, an additional judge would be appointed, subject, of course, to Senate confirmation. The disabled judges then would become junior members of the court and would not be replaced following their death or retirement. The legislation divided the Congress. The measure, nevertheless, passed by 114 votes in the House and five in the Senate with Republicans voting with the majority in both instances. President Wilson subsequently appointed several judges (Samuel Sibley, ND–GA; Edwin Webb, WD–NC) under the provisions of the act.

41. Promotions from Associate to Chief Judge on the Court of Appeals and Supreme Court of the District of Columbia (now the District Court for the District of Columbia) are included in the elevation totals from 1869 through 1932. Analogous to advancements on the U.S. Supreme Court, these within-court promotions created a vacancy and so the opportunity to make an additional appointment. Effective in 1955, the chief judgeship on these courts became based on seniority.

42. Fourteen Republicans joined 39 Democrats in opposing the 1869 resolution. All 90 of the supporters were Republicans.

43. Two of Garfield and Arthur's circuit-level appointments arose from the elevation of Samuel Blatchford, of the Second Circuit, and William Woods, of the Fifth, to the U.S. Supreme Court. Indeed, Blatchford's appointment by Arthur marked the first judicial "trifecta" in U.S. Federal Court History. William J. Wallace of the Northern District Court of New York subsequently filled the vacancy coming from Blatchford's promotion, and Wallace, in turn, was replaced by Alfred Coxe on the Northern District Court. George Bush recently accomplished the feat by naming Judge Souter, of the First Circuit Court of Appeals, to the High Court, elevating Judge Norman Stahl from the District Court of New Hampshire to the vacant position on the First Circuit, and filling Stahl's former position by appointing Stephen McAuliffe. See U.S. Senate, Senate Judiciary Committee, *One Hundred-Second Congress: Calendar of Nominations.*

44. Cleveland made only two circuit-level appointments: Howell Jackson to the Sixth Circuit, and E. Henry LaCombe to the Second. Republicans occupied all the district court positions in these circuits at the time the two were nominated.

45. Act of March 3, 1891 (23 Stat. 826). Two of the appointments were made by Grover Cleveland and William McKinley.

46. The legislation authorizing appellate court restructuring (H.R. 16658) originated in the House, where Republicans held a 42-vote edge. The party's margin was narrower in the Senate (three votes).

47. Cleveland and Wilson faced the same problem in making appointments to the United States Supreme Court, elevating only one of the seven justices they placed on the High Court. Their appointees averaged less than two years prior judicial experience compared to seven and one-half years for the group appointed by Republican presidents.

48. Some of these Democratic judges went to extraordinary lengths to ensure their seats were retained by members of their party. Wilson's election in 1912, for example, marked only the third time in 56 years that a Democrat was elected president. Yet of the seven judges appointed to federal judgeships during Cleveland's two terms and who retired during Wilson's presidency, six were Democrats who had waited an average of 24 years for the event; that is, had waited the equivalent of six presidential terms. The comparable example of service longevity for Republicans during the period of study is held by the 33 judges commissioned by Harding, Coolidge, or Hoover who retired during Eisenhower's presidency. Ninety-one percent ($N = 30$) of this cohort were Republicans whose length of service on the bench averaged 28 years.

49. The number of same-party leavers, 123 versus 35, was equally one-sided.

50. Democrats made only one cross-party appointment, Charles M. Hough of New York, to fill a vacancy on the Second Circuit Court of Appeals in 1916.

51. We find, once again, little difference in this figure by level of court. The cross-party appointment rate was 6 percent for the district courts and 9 percent for the appellate courts.

52. Indeed, Grover Cleveland in his first term extended the practice of appointing Democrats to the U.S. territorial courts, where all but one of the appointments he made ($N = 46$), an unconfirmed recess commission to a judgeship in Montana on the eve of its statehood, went to members of his party. Presidents were virtually unfettered in making appointments to these courts, and as a consequence turnover rates were extraordinarily high. During Cleveland's first term, for instance, all of the Republicans on these courts (27) either resigned ($N = 6$), saw their commissions expire ($N - 13$), or were removed from office ($N = 8$) by Cleveland. Benjamin Harrison, in turn, replaced all of Cleveland's appointees. Four years later Cleveland returned the favor. Congress, by the turn of the century, in an effort to bring some measure of stability to these courts, gradually extended the term of appointment from four to six years, and then to eight or 10 years, allowing service during good behavior and thereby ending executive removal of officeholders. Information on territorial court judgeships and judges, sometimes incomplete, can be found in Clarence Carter, ed., *The Territorial Papers of the United States,* vol. 1 (Washington, D.C.: Government Printing Office, 1934); Edwin Surrency, "The Federal District Court Judges and the History of Their Courts," *Federal Rules Decisions* 103 (1967): 139–310; and *Judges of the United States.* Otherwise consult *Journal of the Executive Proceedings of the Senate of the United States* and *Register of the Department of Justice.*

53. Richard Nixon is the exception. Nixon, nevertheless, was well on his way to carving out a Republican majority on the lower bench when he resigned from the presidency in 1974. The Ford administration, for the record, broke the barrier several months later.

54. When James Buchanan left office in 1861, Democrats held 83 percent of the existing judgeships.

55. Republicans would have held a majority of seats in the House during the 65th Congress, but a number died before it convened, enabling the Democrats, who through this bizarre fluke were now the governing party, to organize the chamber.

Chapter 4

The first epigraph from *Congressional Record,* May 3, 1938, 6180. Kansas happened to be one of the states whose recommendation for a new position was deleted from both the Senate and House versions of the omnibus judgeship bill of 1938. The second epigraph from *Congressional Record,* August 8, 1935, 12743.

1. Democrats realized unified control of government during the 46th, 53d, 63d–65th, and 73d Congresses. The party, which held fewer seats in the House than the GOP in the 65th Congress, nevertheless ran the chamber with the support of several minor parties.

2. Until the 1994 election, Harry Truman was the only Democrat in the post–New Deal era to confront a congress (the 80th) in which the Republicans held a majority of seats in both houses. Republicans predominated in only one other congress, the 83d, during Dwight Eisenhower's first term.

3. Thomas Jefferson's Democratic-Republican Party built on its majority in the 7th Congress during the ensuing three congresses. The party duplicated the trick over the course of the 15th through 18th Congresses during Monroe's presidency. Whereas Roosevelt has the singular distinction among post–Civil War presidents of not suffering the usual midterm decrease in seats held by the president's party in both houses of Congress, nine (Lincoln, Arthur, McKinley, T. Roosevelt (twice), Wilson, F. Roosevelt, Kennedy, and Reagan) since 1860 have seen their party build on majorities in the Senate, the confirming chamber, following off-year elections. Partisan control of the Senate, from the standpoint of the federal judiciary, affects the percentage of same-party appointments to the courts, whereas unified control of both houses affects the rate of bench expansion.

4. See James MacGregor Burns, *Roosevelt: The Lion and the Fox* (New York: Harcourt Brace, 1956); Gregory A. Caldeira, "Public Opinion and the U.S. Supreme Court: FDR's Court Packing Plan," *American Political Science Review* 81 (1987): 1139–53; Sidney M. Milkis, *The President and the Parties: The Transformation of the American Party System Since the New Deal* (New York: Oxford University Press, 1993).

5. The Democratic Party's share of positions on the High Court, courts of appeals, and district courts by the end of Roosevelt's second term were 67 percent, 71 percent, and 52 percent, respectively.

6. The literature on this subject is vast and often controversial. See, for example, John E. Schwarz, *America's Hidden Success* (New York: W. W. Norton, 1988); Herbert Stein, *Presidential Economics: The Making of Economic Policy from Roosevelt to Reagan and Beyond* (Washington, D.C.: American Enterprise Institute for Public Policy Research, 1988); Kevin Phillips, *The Politics of Rich and Poor: Wealth and the American Electorate in the Reagan Aftermath* (New York: HarperCollins, 1990); Michael S. Lewis-Beck and Peverill Squire, "The Transformation of the American State: The New Era-New Deal Test," *Journal of Politics* 53 (1991): 106–21.

7. Prior to 1937 justices who left the Court had to resign rather than retire, so their pensions fluctuated with changes in civil service guidelines. The Supreme Court Retirement Act of 1937 (28 USC 375) allowed judges who were seventy years old with

ten years of continuous service to receive the salary they made at the time of resignation. See Congressional Quarterly, *Guide to the U.S. Supreme Court* (Washington, D.C.: Congressional Quarterly, 1979), 755–56, 774.

8. For purposes of comparison across various subperiods, the 3,455 members of the short-lived Office of Economic Opportunity were excluded from the total. *Statistical Abstract of the United States, 1968* (Washington, D.C.: Government Printing Office, 1969), 396.

9. *Statistical Abstract of the United States 1944,* 179, reports an Executive Office staff of 358 in 1941, the first year in which the Bureau of the Budget is included in the tally.

10. Harrison W. Fox, Jr. and Susan Webb Hammond, *Congressional Staffs: The Invisible Force in American Lawmaking* (New York: The Free Press, 1977), 171.

11. There were 86 judicial districts and 11 circuits in 1933, and 96 and 11 respectively in 1968. Significant changes in the Judicial Code of the United States during the time frame included: authorizing one judicial district each for the states of Alaska (1958) and Hawaii (1959), and the territory of Puerto Rico (1966); creating a new middle district in Florida (1962); reducing the number of districts in South Carolina to one (1965); increasing the number in California to four (1966).

12. The numbers refer to permanent federal judgeships, that is, offices in which successors are authorized, and are based on the Judicial Code of 1911, 1940, 1946, 1952, 1958, 1964, 1970, and various editions of *United States Statutes at Large.* Temporary positions are ones that do not allow a vacancy to be filled in that office or on that court. Congress, nevertheless, rarely fails to convert temporary lines into permanent ones.

13. The two permanent judgeships were for the Fourth Circuit Court of Appeals, the lone appellate court position in the 1922 bill, and the Middle District of Tennessee.

14. Representative Hatton W. Sumners (D–TX), quoting from his own remarks on the 1922 Act. *Congressional Record,* August 8, 1935, 12740.

15. During William Taft's 1922–29 stewardship of the Judicial Conference, for example, 25 judgeships were recommended. Republican-controlled congresses of the era created 41.

16. Officially, Republicans held a two-seat advantage in the lower house following the 1930 elections. Democrats nevertheless organized the chamber because afterward several GOP representatives died in office, enough to swing majority control to the Democrats. See Norman J. Ornstein, Thomas E. Mann, and Michael J. Malbin, *Vital Statistics on Congress, 1989–1990* (Washington, D.C.: Congressional Quarterly, 1990), Table 1-18. See also the *Biographical Directory of the United States Congress, 1774–1989* (Washington, D.C.: Government Printing Office, 1989), 347–52.

17. Peter G. Fish, *The Politics of Federal Judicial Administration* (Princeton, N.J.: Princeton University Press, 1979), 107.

18. The additional judgeships were distributed as follows: two in the Northern District of Illinois, and one apiece in the Southern District of Illinois and Eastern District of Michigan. Additionally, Congress authorized the conversion of a temporary position in the District of New Jersey to a permanent line in 1932.

19. The exceptions were for two seats each in the Southern Districts of California

and New York. U.S. Judiciary, Judicial Conference, *Annual Report of the Judicial Conference of the United States,* September 1934. The figures cited in this chapter for bench expansion are usually slightly higher than those mentioned in sources such as the *Congressional Record* because conversions of temporary to permanent positions are counted in the totals.

20. The Judicial Code authorized one permanent and two temporary judgeships for Massachusetts. The latter positions, legislated by the 1922 act, did not permit successors.

21. Indeed the transcript of the "debate" over the bill in the *Congressional Record* runs to less than a full page.

22. *Congressional Record,* August 8, 1935, 12742.

23. *Congressional Record,* August 8, 1935, 12739.

24. The exception was William A. Pettinger (R–MN), whose state was to receive one of the conversions.

25. McFarlane apparently had no use for the federal judiciary whatsoever:

> The arrogance that has grown up in these lifetime courts and the rottenness of the receiverships appointed under many of these lifetime judges make it clear that the Alexander Hamilton theory of private court for the aristocracy of wealth was and is wrong. . . . It seems to me that we should seriously consider abolishing the Federal district courts and give their jurisdiction to the State courts (*Congressional Record,* August 8, 1935, 12747).

26. Additionally, three members of the Farmer Labor Party voted for the resolution. Among the contingent of Progressive Party affiliates, six voted against the bill and one voted for it.

27. The August 1935 Act, along with its companion, the Act of August 2, authorized 20 permanent positions, 4 more than requested by the Judicial Conference. The 75th and 76th Congresses subsequently added 37 permanent positions, all but 5 new, and 13 temporary lines. The judgeship lists of the Judicial Conference, by comparison, called for 30 permanent positions and 3 temporary ones, once again illustrating that congresses governed by the president's party typically exceed Conference recommendations.

28. Actually three of the district judgeships were temporary. The bill also provided for the conversion of a temporary judgeship in Montana attendant upon filling the next vacancy, and fixed the number of judges on the Court of Appeals for the Third Circuit at five. In neither case were new judgeships created.

29. The sixteen judgeships were distributed as follows: three for the District of Columbia and one each for the Second, Fifth, Sixth, and Seventh Circuits, Southern District of California, the Northern District of Georgia, Eastern District of Louisiana, Western District of Louisiana, District of Kansas, Eastern District of Michigan, Northern District of Ohio, Southern District of Texas, and Western District of Washington.

30. *Congressional Record,* March 30, 1938, 4350.

31. Addressing his minority colleagues on the matter, Warren R. Austin (R–VT) characterized the committee's efforts thusly:

> No consideration of partisanship or politics entered into the study of the problem. It was handled as a national problem, from a purely patriotic point of view. So far as I know, no question of partisanship ever entered into the consideration of the bill at any time (*Congressional Record,* March 25, 1938, 4135).

32. The Judiciary Committee dropped the Judicial Conference's recommendations for new seats in the Eastern District of Louisiana, Northern District of Ohio, District of Kansas, and one of the three for the District Court of the District of Columbia. The committee, upon the recommendation of the attorney general, added positions in the District of Columbia Circuit, the Northern District of California, the Northern District of Illinois, the Southern District of New York, the Western District of Virginia, the Eastern/Western District of Arkansas, and the Eastern/Middle/Western District of Tennessee.

33. Typical of this point of view are the remarks of Senator William H. King (D–UT):

> Some of the judges provided for in the bill obviously should be appointed. Assignments are made in some districts where none should be made. A sort of mania or hysteria for more judges and more court procedure has infected many of our States. I shall not single out some of the districts where I think no judges should be named. I have in mind the fact that the judicial conferences which met a year ago and two years ago recommended not more than four or five judges. . . . However, we have transcended the view and recommendation of the judicial conference and have introduced a bill which, in my opinion, provides for the appointment of too many judges (*Congressional Record,* March 30, 1938, 4357).

34. An exception was the dialogue between the senators from New York, both Democrats yet split on the need for a new position in the Southern District of New York. Senator Royal S. Copeland saw no need for a new permanent position, arguing instead that caseload pressures—in general and certainly in the case of this court—were episodic and could best be addressed by utilizing visiting judges from other districts. After all,

> I think almost any judge on any occasion should be glad to serve in New York, but when a world's fair is being held there a judge certainly should be more pleased than ever to come to New York.

The problem, as he saw it, was that the $5 per diem for visiting judges served as a disincentive, one that could be corrected by raising it to $10. Senator Robert Wagner disagreed, defending his claim for an additional judgeship with statistics and the testimony before the committee by judges from the court. *Congressional Record,* March 30, 1938, 4351. Roosevelt, in all probability, placed greater stock in Wagner's view on the matter, as he was a New Deal loyalist and an insider in Democratic circles. Copeland, on the other hand, a physician by training, was somewhat out of the mainstream of the party.

35. Votes from the Farmer Labor (two "yea"), Progressive (one "yea"), and Independent-Republican Parties (one "nay") made up the remainder.

36. The remarks of Thomas D. P. O'Malley (D–WI) cut to the heart of the matter:

> If some of these plutocrats of the bench would get down to work at 9 o'clock and work the same hours as a Member of Congress and all other Government employees, additional judges would not be needed and this tremendous additional burden on our distressed taxpayers would not be necessary (*Congressional Record,* March 3, 1938, 6200).

37. Perhaps the most vocal (and certainly the longest-winded) critic was Earl C. Michener (R–MI). Layered upon his criticism of the bill was a veneer of deference to the wisdom of the Judicial Conference:

> Where the recommendations of the conference have been followed, no political judgeships have been created, and I cannot recall a single instance where time has not proved the wisdom of the conference recommendations.

Michener proceeded to offer separate amendments for each clause of the bill that provided for a position not recommended by the Judicial Conference; each one was the subject of considerable discussion, especially by representatives whose states would gain a seat. *Congressional Record,* May 3, 1938, 6177.

38. *Congressional Record,* May 17, 1938, 6983, 7005.

39. The bill represented a genuine compromise between the two versions. For example, the House receded to the Senate version that did not contain positions for the Northern District of Ohio and the district of New Jersey, whereas the Senate reciprocated to the House bill that had a third position for the D.C. District and converted the next vacancy in a temporary position in Montana to permanent. Both chambers had new seats for the Northern and the Southern districts of California. The House bill stipulated that the occupant of the new seat in the Northern District would have to reside in Sacramento, and Fresno would be the home base of the Southern seat. The rationale was that all the other judges in the Northern District sat in San Francisco, whereas their Southern District colleagues lived in Los Angeles, placing a burden on citizens who resided in those districts but far from the two hub cities (by as much as three hundred miles in the southern district). The Senate conferees consented to compromise language that required the judge to have judicial residence in the named cities but not necessarily live there.

40. Jesse Summer (R–IL) expressed the pipe dream thusly

> It seems to me that the question ought to be commented on whether it is better to appoint these judges now or wait, perhaps, until the next Congress or the next administration comes in. It seems to me that always before this administration, Presidents of both parties have appointed independent men and able lawyers as judges, and it might be, we hope, that the next administration, regardless of party, will adopt that traditional policy (*Congressional Record,* March 14, 1940, 2901).

41. An exception was Representative John C. Schafer (R–WI), who flippantly proposed an amendment to create a new position in the Virgin Islands on these grounds

> I believe that after the New Deal goes out with the wind in November and New Deal Federal bureaucratic tyranny is ended we will be able to reduce the number of judgeships we already have. I offer this amendment to create a judgeship in the Virgin Islands so that you can find a good "lame duck" berth for an expert on the Virgin Islands, Prof. Rex Tugwell, so that when the New Deal goes out in 1940 he can go back to the Virgin Islands and dispense his pure conceptions of Karl Marx socialism (*Congressional Record,* March 14, 1940, 2909).

42. Although the Conference recommended only one position for the Eighth Circuit in its 1939 report, the Judiciary Committee offered an amendment to add a second since conditions had changed since then, owing primarily to the increasing infirmity of one of the judges. *Congressional Record,* March 14, 1940, 2891.

43. *Congressional Record,* March 14, 1940, 2911–12.

44. *Congressional Record,* April 15, 1940, 4494.

45. The Senate version contained a position for the Northern and Southern Districts of Florida not in the House bill and omitted seats in the Northern Districts of Georgia and Illinois that the House authorized.

46. *Congressional Record,* May 15, 1940, 6202–3, 6213; May 1, 1940, 7313.

47. Temporary positions were authorized for the Northern District of Ohio, the Eastern and Western Districts of Missouri, and the District of Kansas. A temporary position on the District of New Jersey (1940) was recreated as such (1942). Conversion to permanent status occurred for temporary judgeships in the District of Massachusetts, the Northern District of Alabama, the Northern District of California, the District of New Jersey, and the Eastern District of Pennsylvania. Permanent lines were legislated for the Third and Fifth Circuit Courts of Appeals.

48. Relations between the new chief executive and the membership of the 79th Congress apparently were strained as well. During this span only four additional positions were authorized: in the Northern District of California; the District of Kansas; the Eastern District of Pennsylvania; and the Eastern, Middle, and Western Districts of Pennsylvania, the latter being a roving judgeship. Moreover, Congress gave Truman only 90 days to forward a nominee for the multidistrict position, otherwise the authorization would expire (Act of July 24, 1946). Lastly the permanent judgeship for the Eastern District of Pennsylvania merely clarified the authorization under a previous act, that of December 7, 1944.

49. Earl C. Michener (R–MI) and Edward H. Rees (R–KS). In the words of the latter

> With the distinguished gentleman from Michigan [Mr. Michener], I am also one of those who is wary with regard to additional charges to the Federal Treasury. This charge, however, in my judgment, is not only necessary, but will result in savings by reason of more expeditious hearings in our courts (*Congressional Record,* June 16, 1949, 7843).

50. The Judicial Conference asked for five permanent and one temporary circuit positions, seventeen permanent and two temporary district positions, and four conversions on the district courts. *Report of the Proceedings of the Judicial Conference of the United States,* Special Session March 24–25, 1949, 196–97.

51. *Congressional Record,* June 16, 1949, 7856.

52. Floor debate focused almost entirely on a Judiciary Committee amendment, tendered by the chair, Patrick A. McCarran (D–NV), placing restrictions on the three appointments to the D.C. District Court. All three "shall not have been regularly employed in the executive branch of the Government of the United States, during a period of at least three consecutive years immediately prior to their respective appointments," and "at least two shall have been actively engaged in the private practice of law in the District of Columbia for a period of at least five consecutive years immediately prior to their respective appointments." The intent of the first part of the amendment was to prevent situations where judges would preside over cases in which citizens were contesting the actions of federal agencies for or with whom the judges had worked. The intent of the second was to tighten the local connection of D.C. judges who heretofore did not have to reside in the D.C. area. *Congressional Record,* June 27, 1949, 8412.

53. The Judicial Conference requested the conversion of a temporary seat in the Eastern and Western Districts of Missouri that the conference committee ignored, whereas the latter recommended a conversion in the Western District of Oklahoma that the Judicial Conference did not mention.

54. Congress created new permanent judgeships for the Fourth Circuit Court of Appeals and the Southern District Court of Texas, positions designated as temporary by the Judicial Conference. Additionally, no action was taken on the recommendation to convert to permanent the temporary judgeship for the Eastern and Western District Court of Missouri, whereas Congress did authorize a conversion for the Western District of Oklahoma, a district not targeted by the Conference.

55. *Congressional Quarterly Almanac, 1949,* (Washington, D.C.: Congressional Quarterly, 1950), 573.

56. Actually this bill, in addition to expanding the bench, included a number of other provisions having to do with retirement options, redrawing the jurisdictional lines of the district courts, changing the terms of territorial judges, and stipulating the residences of judges within certain districts. As such it was an important event not only for bench expansion, but for judicial administration in general.

57. The Conference recommended 4 new (and permanent) appeals court judgeships and 33 on the district courts. Judgeships on the latter courts would include 6 temporary positions, 4 conversions, and 23 new and permanent lines. *Report of the Proceedings of the Judicial Conference of the United States,* September 24, 1953, 6–8.

58. Republicans in the 83d Congress held slim majorities of 10 seats in the House and 2 in the Senate.

59. Arthur G. Klein (D–NY), expressed it this way:

> I believe that this action on the part of this Republican-controlled Congress is purely political. This bill, or one very similar to it, was reported out and came up

> for a vote on the floor of this House in the 82d Congress. Most of the Members who are now advocating its passage opposed it at that time for frankly political reasons. They felt that in the coming presidential election there was a possibility that a Republican President would be elected. In that event, appointments to the Federal judiciary would be made by the new Republican President (*Congressional Record,* February 3, 1954, 1270).

60. One amendment was approved to create an extra seat in the District of Puerto Rico, but ultimately it was deleted from the conference committee version of the bill.

61. *Congressional Record,* July 30, 1953, 10581.

62. Witness the remark of John Dingell (D–MI), *Congressional Record,* July 30, 1953, 10587: "We could, in fact better use 2 additional judges in the eastern district [of Michigan] than to have an increase of 1 in the western district."

63. With reference to these two positions Celler argued (*Congressional Record,* February 3, 1954, 1266): "Judged by usual standards I will say beyond peradventure of doubt that there is no more need for any additional judge in those two States than there is need for any one of you gentlemen to have a hole in your head." Representative Thomas J. Lane (D–MA) also entered into the record the transcript of a telegram received from Utah Governor J. Bracken Lee (*Congressional Record,* February 3, 1954, 1265): "The bill which provides for an additional district judge in Utah is the same type of graft that the Republicans so severely criticized the Democrats for in the past."

64. The other position came from converting a temporary judgeship in the District of South Dakota from Eisenhower's 1954 bill to permanent status in 1957.

65. The decline in Eisenhower's legislative fortunes is easy to trace. During the 83d Congress, for example, support in Congress for bills favored by the administration was 86 percent; six years later it was 59 percent. *Vital Statistics on American Politics,* table 8-11.

66. The Administrative Office of the United States Courts was created by the Act of August 7, 1939 (28 U.S.C 601). The director and deputy director are appointed by the chief justice after consultation with the Judicial Conference. Chandler, incidentally, was a Republican.

67. *Report of the Proceedings of the Annual Meeting of the Judicial Conference of the United States,* September 19, 1955, 83–84.

68. *Report of the Proceedings of the Annual Meeting of the Judicial Conference of the United States,* September 19, 1956, 2–3.

69. *Report of the Proceedings of the Annual Meeting of the Judicial Conference of the United States,* September 17, 1958, 66.

70. Olney was a Republican.

71. Olney also was instructed by and cited the remarks of his immediate superior, the Chief Justice of the United States, Earl Warren. Addressing a meeting of the American Bar Association, Warren challenged the judiciary to make: "the administration of justice the great central cause of our profession." *Report of the Proceedings of the Annual Meeting of the Judicial Conference of the United States,* September 17, 1958, 67.

72. Text of letter reprinted in *Congressional Quarterly Weekly Report,* February 17, 1961, 296.

73. *Congressional Quarterly Weekly Report,* February 17, 1961, 263.

74. *Congressional Quarterly Weekly Report,* March 10, 1961, 385.

75. *Congressional Quarterly Weekly Report,* March 10, 1961, 385.

76. *Congressional Quarterly Weekly Report,* March 10, 1961, 385.

77. *Congressional Quarterly Weekly Report,* April 21, 1961, 662.

78. *Congressional Quarterly Weekly Report,* May 5, 1961, 756. PL 87-36 authorized 70 new and permanent judgeships, converted 4 temporary lines into permanent ones, transferred another, and mandated an additional term, federal judgeship for the District of Puerto Rico.

79. Democrats outnumbered Republicans 295 to 140 in the House, and 68 to 32 in the Senate of the 89th Congress.

80. The alternating format held through the Nixon administration, which received authorization under PL 90-347 to appoint only district court judges to new positions. Nixon, nevertheless, named several appointees to new appellate court judgeships that had carried over from Johnson's bill.

81. *Congressional Quarterly Weekly Report,* July 9, 1965.

82. *Congressional Quarterly Weekly Report,* March 11, 1966, 550. The bill ultimately became PL 89-372.

83. Congress failed to authorize an additional judgeship for the Southern District of Georgia, provided for three new positions for the Central District of California rather than the two called for, added additional positions for the Eighth Circuit and the Northern District of Mississippi, and subsequently, under PL 89-571, converted the two term judgeships in the District of Puerto Rico into Article III positions.

84. The positions were distributed as follows: one each for the Third and Tenth Circuits; six for the Fifth, with four coming from converting temporary judgeships into permanent lines; and four for the Ninth. *Report of the Proceedings of the Judicial Conference of the United States,* March 30–31, 1967, 9.

85. The additional judgeship legislated by Congress went to the Sixth Circuit Court of Appeals.

86. See chapter 6 herein.

87. The omnibus judgeship bill of 1961 (PL 87-6), for example, authorized additional positions for 32 of the 50 states. Only 10 states were so deprived in the 1978 bill (PL 95-486).

88. All but two of the cross-party appointees to the courts of appeals were elevated during the 1933–68 era. Their replacements were almost always same-party members. The two exceptions were Robert P. Patterson, for whose position on the Southern District Court of New York no successor was authorized, and Francis Van Dusen, on the Eastern District Court of Pennsylvania, whose successor was John Hannum, a Nixon appointee.

89. Appointments to the courts of appeals are not immune, of course, from the influence of individual senators, especially when a judge from the state they represent leaves the appellate bench. During the 1933–68 era half of the cross-party appointees alone came from the same state as their predecessors. Overall, 68.4 percent of the time

the successor's and predecessor's home state were the same. Carrying the analysis one step further, in instances where the successor came from a different state, 60 percent of the time there were more same-party senators from the appointee's home state than there were from the predecessor's, 23 percent of the time the number was the same, and in the remainder there were fewer.

90. One of the appointees, Floyd Roberts, Republican, of the Western District Court of Virginia, was given a recess appointment by Roosevelt in 1938. The nominee failed confirmation and the position went to a Democrat. Eisenhower and Johnson's partisan appointment rates were at or near the norm. Kennedy's was below average owing to the sprinkling of Republicans appointed to new positions in the wake of the record-shattering omnibus judgeship bill of 1961 or otherwise to fill vacancies in such Republican strongholds as California, Kansas, Iowa, Illinois, Indiana, and New York. The tally includes two of Eisenhower's unconfirmed, recess appointees, Caffrey (District of Massachusetts) and Tavares (District of Hawaii), who were subsequently renominated by Kennedy and confirmed by the 87th Congress. Perhaps with a record number of new positions to fill, Kennedy could afford to dispense with partisan considerations, at least in these two instances. Parenthetically, most of Truman's cross-party appointments were made in the year of the 1949 omnibus judgeship act.

91. Resignees comprised 9.7 percent of the total. Nearly two of every three (61 percent) of those retiring during the era did so after 1952, that is, in the second half of the subperiod.

92. There is no appreciable difference by level of court: the same-party leaving rate on the courts of appeals is 56 percent, and only one percentage point higher on the district courts.

93. There were three Eisenhower appointees who resigned or retired during his administration. They are not included in the length-of-service figures.

94. Three of the elevations were promotions from associate to chief judge on the District of Columbia District and Circuit Courts. The advancements, nonetheless, created an associate judgeship vacancy and so an opportunity to make a second appointment. Effective in 1955 on the D.C. Court of Appeals and 1958 on the District Court, the position of chief judge was determined by seniority.

95. The strategy can backfire, of course. A cross-party appointee might fundamentally change his or her decision making once he or she has moved to a higher court with new colleagues. The same is true, however, of judges of the president's party.

96. See, for example, U.S. Judiciary, Judicial Conference, *The Quiet Crisis: A Report by the 1984–85 Commission on Executive, Legislative, and Judicial Salaries* (Washington, D.C.: Government Printing Office, 1985); U.S. Judiciary, Judicial Conference, *Simple Fairness: The Case for Equitable Compensation of the Nation's Federal Judges* (Washington, D.C.: Government Printing Office, 1988).

Chapter 5

First epigraph from Kevin P. Phillips, *The Emerging Republican Majority* (New York: Anchor Books, 1970), 25; see also Richard M. Scammon and Ben J. Wattenberg, *The Real Majority* (New York: Coward-McCann, 1970). Second epigraph from *Congressional Quarterly Weekly Report,* February 11, 1978, 369.

1. See, for example, Norman H. Nie, Sidney Verba, and John R. Petrocik, *The Changing American Voter* (Cambridge, Mass.: Harvard University Press, 1976).

2. For a discussion of trends at the subnational level, see Malcolm E. Jewell and David M. Olson, *Political Parties and Elections in American States,* 3d ed. (Chicago: Dorsey Press, 1988).

3. Randall B. Ripley, *Congress: Process and Policy,* 4th ed. (N.Y.: W.W. Norton & Company, 1988), 76.

4. See Lawrence C. Dodd and Richard L. Schott, *Congress and the Administrative State* (New York: John Wiley and Sons, 1979).

5. Norman J. Ornstein, Thomas E. Mann, and Michael J. Malbin, *Vital Statistics on Congress, 1993–1994* (Washington, D.C.: Congressional Quarterly Press, 1994), 126–27. This figure does not include the 6,254 positions in the four congressional staff agencies—the Congressional Budget Office, the General Accounting Office, the Office of Technology Assessment, and the Congressional Research Service. These were excluded from the calculations to standardize comparisons across subperiods—two of the four agencies were created after 1968, during which time the other two experienced moderate growth.

6. See Richard P. Nathan, *The Administrative Presidency* (New York: John Wiley & Sons, 1983).

7. See Harold Seidman and Robert Gilmour, *Politics, Position and Power,* 4th ed. (New York: Oxford University Press, 1986); Stephen Hess, *Organizing the Presidency* (Washington, D.C.: Brookings Institution, 1988).

8. Regarding the evolution of the Bureau of Budget to the Office of Management and Budget, see Larry Berman, *The Office of Management and Budget and the Presidency, 1921–1979* (Princeton, N.J.: Princeton University Press, 1979).

9. *Statistical Abstract of the United States, 1993* (Washington, D.C.: Government Printing Office, 1993), 343.

10. This episode in judicial administration is chronicled in Deborah J. Barrow and Thomas G. Walker, *A Court Divided* (New Haven, Conn.: Yale University Press, 1988).

11. *Judicial Code of the United States,* 1968, 1992. Additionally, a territorial court in the Northern Mariana Islands opened in January 1979, and the District of the Canal Zone closed in March 1982.

12. Created by the Act of December 20, 1967, 28 U.S.C. 620. The Center's policies and activities are determined by its board, by statute composed of: the chief justice (chair), two appeals court judges, three district court judges, three district judges, one bankruptcy judge, and the director of the Administrative Office of the United States Courts. The chief justice and the Administrative Office director are permanent members of the board; the others are elected for four-year terms by the Judicial Conference.

13. See the discussion in chapter 3 herein and more generally in Peter G. Fish, *The Politics of Federal Judicial Administration* (Princeton, N.J.: Princeton University Press, 1973).

14. This figure includes only Article III judges, and excludes judges from the Federal Circuit as well as territorial positions (e.g., District Court of the Virgin Islands). At the close of the Bush administration, 90 district and 17 appeals court judgeships were vacant. See U.S. Judiciary, Administrative Office of the United States Courts, *Third Branch* 25 (1993), 11.

15. This represents a 79.3 percent increase for the appeals courts and a 71.2 percent increase in the district courts.

16. The Judicial Conference typically made yearly recommendations for new judgeships from 1922 to 1948, biannual requests from then to 1964, quadrennial requests from 1964 to 1977, and has made biennial requests ever since.

17. *Report of the Proceedings of the Judicial Conference of the United States,* September 19–20, 1968, 50–51. The recommendations called for converting five temporary positions into permanent ones, including transferring a roving judgeship on the Middle and Southern Districts of Alabama to the Southern District of the state, adding 63 new and permanent lines, and adding one temporary judgeship.

18. All told 25 states, notably those having multidistricts, and the territory of Puerto Rico were to receive additional judgeships under PL 91-272.

19. The 1970 bill created 57 new and permanent positions, three conversions, three temporary lines, and one transfer. The Kennedy bill allowed 3 more permanent positions, an additional conversion, and one less temporary judgeship.

20. Note the roll call votes in the House on PL 89-372 (see chap. 4) and PL 91-272, passed in 1966 and 1970, respectively. The partisan breakdown among those voting for these bills representing states not in line to receive new judgeships shows 82 percent Republican during Johnson's administration (1966) and 90 percent Democrat during Nixon's (1970).

21. *Report of the Proceedings of the Judicial Conference of the United States,* October 28–29, 1971, 81.

22. *Report of the Proceedings of the Judicial Conference of the United States,* October 26–27, 1972, 34–35. One of the 52 recommended positions converted a temporary line into a permanent one.

23. *Report of the Proceedings of the Judicial Conference of the United States,* September 19–20, 1974, 43.

24. *Congressional Quarterly Weekly Report,* October 4, 1975, 2130; October 11, 1975, 2175; August 21, 1976, 2280.

25. Following the national elections of 1976, Democrats enjoyed a 149-vote majority in the House, and a 23-vote advantage in the Senate.

26. *Congressional Quarterly Weekly Report,* May 21, 1977, 987; May 28, 1977, 1069.

27. *Report of the Proceedings of the Judicial Conference of the United States,* March 10–11, 1977, 5–6. At this session the Conference also moved from a quadrennial to a biennial format for its judgeship surveys. See Jon Bond, "The Politics of Court Structure: The Addition of New Federal Judges," *Law and Policy Quarterly* 2 (1980): 181–88 for an analysis of omnibus judgeship legislation from the Truman through the Carter administrations.

28. See Barrow and Walker, *A Court Divided,* for a complete analysis of the

importance of additional judgeships to the administration of justice, and the impact of politics on the 1978 bill as well as the proposal to divide the Fifth Circuit.

29. *Congressional Quarterly Weekly Report,* November 19, 1977, 2443.

30. *Congressional Quarterly Weekly Report,* December 3, 1977, 2519–20. Parenthetically, this bill contained no provision for the splitting of the Fifth Circuit. See Larry C. Berkson and Susan Carbon, *The United States Circuit Judge Nominating Commission* (Chicago: American Judicature Society, 1981), and Alan Neff, *The United States District Judge Nominating Commissions* (Chicago: American Judicature Society, 1980) for full discussion and evaluation of the merit-based proposals.

31. The division occurred two years later. See PL 96-452.

32. *Congressional Quarterly Weekly Report,* October 14, 1978, 2961–62.

33. *Congressional Quarterly Weekly Report,* December 3, 1977, 2520.

34. For an excellent analysis of federal bankruptcy procedures through the mid-1970s see Carroll Seron, *Judicial Reorganization* (Lexington, Mass.: Lexington Books, 1978).

35. *Northern Pipeline Co. v. Marathon Pipe Line,* 102 S.Ct. 2858 (1982).

36. For background see *Congressional Quarterly Weekly Report,* April 10, 1982, 806; July 3, 1982, 1572; July 7, 1984, 1665–67.

37. Democrats had a 102-vote majority in the House during the 98th Congress.

38. *Report of the Proceedings of the Judicial Conference of the United States,* September 22–23, 1982, 61–62, 88. Subsequently in March 1983 the Conference raised the number of requested appellate court judgeships to 24 (*Report of the Proceedings of the Judicial Conference of the United States,* March 16–17, 1983, 28). The recommended number of bankruptcy judgeships was pegged at 305 at the September 1983 session (*Report of the Proceedings of the Judicial Conference of the United States,* September 21–22, 1983, 69–70).

39. For background see *Congressional Quarterly Weekly Report,* April 30, 1983, 829–30; March 24, 1984, 646–47; April 14, 1984, 849; May 26, 1984, 1227.

40. PL 98-353 authorized 24 new circuit court positions, 61 district court positions, of which 8 would be temporary, and converted 2 temporary lines to permanent status. The Judicial Conference recommended number of positions varied only in the number of new and permanent district court judgeships, calling for 45 rather than 53.

41. *Congressional Quarterly Weekly Report,* July 7, 1984, 1665–67.

42. *Congressional Quarterly Weekly Report,* November 17, 1990, 3873.

43. *Congressional Quarterly Weekly Report,* November 17, 1990, 3873–77.

44. Ten districts were set aside for a pilot program under which congressional guidelines for accelerating case disposition would be implemented. See *Congressional Quarterly Weekly Report,* November 17, 3873.

45. *Report of the Proceedings of the Judicial Conference of the United States,* September 14, 1988, 86–88; March 13, 1990, 10; September 12, 1990, 57–59.

46. Democrats in the 101st Congress enjoyed sizable majorities of 85 seats in the House and 10 in the Senate.

47. See Jon R. Bond, "The Politics of Court Structure"; Gary Zuk, Gerard S. Gryski, and Deborah J. Barrow, "Partisan Transformation of the Federal Judiciary, 1869–1992," *American Politics Quarterly* 21 (1993): 439–57.

48. *Congressional Quarterly Weekly Report,* December 3, 1977, 2519. In quoting this individual, CQ referred to him or her as "one source familiar with the history of the legislation."

49. We can also report some preliminary evidence on the differential pork barrel politics for new seats versus replacements. During this subperiod 50 percent of the cross-party appointments to new seats under divided government went to states in which both senators were of the party opposite the president, and six of the other seven such seats went to states where one senator was of the opposite party. Under unified government (Carter), 15 of the 21 cross-party appointments to new seats went to states that had at least one Republican senator (three states had two). For replacement seats, under divided government, 12 of 44 went to states with two Democratic senators and another 28 to states with one Democratic senator. Of the four cross-party appointments to replacement seats made by Jimmy Carter, two went to states where both senators were Republicans, and the other two to states with one Republican senator.

50. See the Commission on Executive, Legislative, and Executive Salaries, *The Quiet Crisis: Report of the Commission on Executive, Legislative, and Judicial Salaries* (Washington, D.C.: Government Printing Office, 1984–85); Deborah J. Barrow and Gary Zuk, "An Institutional Analysis of Turnover in the Lower Federal Courts, 1900–1987," *Journal of Politics* 52 (1990): 457–77. Barrow and Zuk in their study of voluntary departures from the lower federal courts during this century found that salary hikes, the measure often recommended by the Quadrennial Commission and by federal judges as the means to dampening turnover, in and of themselves had little to no impact. Judicial leaving behavior continues to be driven by emoluments to the retirement package, along with political factors such as party affiliation of the president.

51. Approximately 18 judges resigned or retired annually during Nixon's presidency. The figure climbed to 32 for the Bush administration.

52. Given the brevity of Ford's administration, one might argue that data for the Ford years should be added to Nixon's for one composite measure. We opted instead to distinguish the two in order to present information in as detailed a manner as possible. Parenthetically, had the two been merged, the Republican leaving rate would have been 51.8 percent, a slim majority, but one nonetheless. The lower partisan leaving rate under Ford could also be a consequence of a number of Democratic judges anticipating Carter's election and so retiring at the close of court. The Democratically controlled Senate would not act, of course, to fill vacancies until the next year. Nearly 30 percent (27.8 percent) of those who left under Ford were replaced by Carter. Sixty-seven percent of the total were Democrats.

53. While drawing the pool on the basis of party is fairly straightforward, one might question whether the state is the appropriate geographic unit, in that the custom of courtesy does not extend with equal vigor to the courts of appeals level. In fact, however, replacement appointments generally go to the states that had the original seat. Furthermore, it would be difficult to construct the pool on the basis of the entire circuit because that would obscure the finer gradations in the data.

54. See Sheldon Goldman, "Bush's Judicial Legacy: The Final Imprint," *Judicature* 76 (1993): 282–97.

55. In some cases the results should be read with caution, given the small numbers

on which the percentages are based. The extreme case is the Ford administration, which made only 11 appointments to the courts of appeals (8 by elevation, and 3 from outside the bench).

56. Again, caution should be exercised in interpreting the percentages, as the numbers on which they are based can be small.

57. See Goldman, "Bush's Judicial Legacy."

58. See Susan Haire, Gerard S. Gryski, Gary Zuk, and Deborah J. Barrow, "An Intercircuit Profile of Judges on the U.S. Courts of Appeals," *Judicature* 78 (1994): 101–3.

59. Looked at another way, the appointment opportunities coming from percent change increases in the bench size are a function of the size of the bench itself. Comparing the last two administrations in the second subperiod (Kennedy and Johnson) and the last two in the third (Reagan and Bush), for example, the bench grew almost four times more (15 versus 4 percent), in the former but yielded only 33 judges versus 56 in the latter.

60. Reagan (and Bush) appointees were also slightly younger at the time of their appointments, so their influence on the bench is likely to endure. Although the differences are not striking, the mean age at appointment for Nixon, Ford, and Carter judges was 51, but was only 49 for Reagan and Bush.

61. There were 107 unfilled vacancies—17 on the appellate bench and 90 on the district bench—when Bush left office in January 1993, more than two times the number (48) at the start of his term, and the largest in the history of the federal courts.

62. Moreover, Nixon was more successful than any president except FDR in "packing" the Supreme Court.

63. An even stronger, albeit conjectural, case can be made for Nixon's influence on the bench. Let us assume that he completed his second term, received the 61 replacement opportunities filled by Ford, and made appointments at his, rather than Ford's, cross-party rate (see table 5.3). The outcome would be a bench 55.9 percent Republican, and Nixon would have altered the partisan balance by 26.1 percent, which is higher than the corresponding mark for Reagan.

64. The change would have been still greater if not for Carter's low same-party appointment rate (see table 5.7), which was uncharacteristic for a president serving under unified government.

Chapter 6

First epigraph from Peter G. Fish, *The Politics of Federal Judicial Administration* (Princeton, N.J.: Princeton University Press, 1973), 12. Judge Adrian A. Spears (WD–TX), recalling the advice given by Vice President Lyndon Johnson, who had been instrumental in securing his close friend's appointment. Second epigraph from a transcript, Adrian A. Spears Oral History Interview, June 11, 1971, 21, Lyndon Baines Johnson Library, as quoted in Neil D. McFeeley, *Appointment of Judges: The Johnson Presidency* (Austin: University of Texas Press, 1987), 78.

1. The figures are calculated as the average for all congresses from 1869 to 1992 (overall), and in the three respective subperiods.

2. See Gerard S. Gryski, Gary Zuk, and Deborah J. Barrow, "A Bench That Looks Like America? The Representation of African-Americans and Latinos on the Federal Courts," *Journal of Politics* 56 (1994): 1076–86.

3. Only Woodrow Wilson, Grover Cleveland (first term), and Ulysses Grant registered lower elevation rates.

4. G. E. P. Box and G. M. Jenkins, *Time Series Analysis: Forecasting and Control* (San Francisco: Holden-Day, 1976). See also G. E. P. Box and G. C. Tiao, "Intervention Analysis with Applications to Economic and Environmental Problems," *Journal of the American Statistical Association* 70 (1975): 70–79. For recent time-series applications in the field of judicial politics, see Deborah J. Barrow and Gary Zuk, "An Institutional Analysis of Turnover in the Lower Federal Courts, 1900–1987," *Journal of Politics* 52 (1990): 457–76; Reginald S. Sheehan, William Mishler, and Donald R. Songer, "Ideology, Status, and the Differential Success of Direct Parties before the Supreme Court," *American Political Science Review* 86 (1992): 464–71; Gary Zuk, Gerard S. Gryski, and Deborah J. Barrow, "Partisan Transformation of the Federal Judiciary, 1869–1992," *American Politics Quarterly* 21 (1993): 439–57. Controversy continues among time-series analysts over the differencing procedure typically used to remedy nonstationarity. Currently so-called error correction models are advanced as a better method of dealing with the problem. See Harold D. Clarke and Marianne C. Stewart, "Prospections, Retrospections, and Rationality: The 'Bankers' Model of Presidential Approval Reconsidered," *American Journal of Political Science* 38 (1994): 1104–23; and Harold D. Clarke and Marianne C. Stewart, "Economic Evaluations, Prime Ministerial Approval and Governing Party Support: Rival Models Reconsidered," *British Journal of Political Science* 25 (1995): 145–70. In our case the data are stationary and so the conventional Box-Jenkins treatment was used. Serial correlation was not a problem either. Residuals were within +/− two standard deviations of mean zero, as required.

5. The average increase in caseload ranged from 0.3 to 118 percent.

6. Bench size during Republican administrations averaged about 12 percent from 1869 to 1932, 9 percentage points higher than that for Democrats. Indeed, of 24 congresses associated with above average growth, 18 came during Republican presidencies, 13 transpiring before the New Deal.

7. Nelson W. Polsby, "The Institutionalization of the U.S. House of Representatives," *American Political Science Review* 62 (1968): 144–68.

8. Polsby, "The Institutionalization of the U.S. House of Representatives," 145.

9. Permeability is a characteristic that has been used successfully in the study of the institutional environment of congressional committees. See especially Richard F. Fenno, Jr., *Congressmen in Committees* (Boston: Little, Brown and Company, 1973).

10. From *Growth of British Policy,* as quoted in *The Oxford Dictionary of Quotations,* 2d ed. (London: Oxford University Press, 1959), 421.

11. See, for example, Walter Dean Burnham, *Critical Elections and the Mainsprings of American Politics* (New York: W. W. Norton & Company, 1970).

12. Two notable exceptions, of course, were the sizable complement of circuit judgeships legislated in 1869 to mitigate "circuit riding" by justices of the U.S. Supreme Court, and the contingent coming with implementation of the Act of 1891 creating the courts of appeals.

13. Two different approaches to studying agenda setting emphasizing its importance to political outcomes are Peter Bachrach, *The Theory of Democratic Elitism* (Boston: Little, Brown and Company, 1967); and Roger W. Cobb and Charles D. Elder, *Participation in American Politics: The Dynamics of Agenda-Building* (Baltimore: Johns Hopkins University Press, 1983).

14. See, for example, Guy Benveniste, *The Politics of Expertise,* 2d ed. (San Francisco: Boyd & Fraser Publishing Company, 1977); Gerard S. Gryski, *Bureaucratic Policy Making in a Technological Society* (Cambridge, Mass.: Schenkman Publishing Company, 1981); and Francis E. Rourke, *Bureaucracy, Politics, and Public Policy,* 3d ed. (Boston: Little, Brown and Company, 1984). A compelling theoretical treatment of this topic can be found in Roberto Mangabeira Unger, *Knowledge and Politics* (New York: The Free Press, 1975). The interplay of politics and knowledge was also an undercurrent in David Halberstam, *The Best and the Brightest* (New York: Random House, 1972).

15. In addition to traditional studies of political institutions, political scientists have recently focused on endogenous factors that influence the development of institutions. See the works cited in chapter 1.

16. Other informal institutional norms are manifest in the question of same- versus cross-party appointments. At the most basic level, the expectation is that presidents will stock the courts with their partisan compatriots, as this is one of the spoils of the presidential election. Some have observed the Senate to be more tolerant of this when a party is reinstated in the White House after an extended absence and faces a partisan imbalance on the bench. See Evan A. Evans, "Political Influence in the Selection of Federal Judges," *Wisconsin Law Review* (1948): 330–51.

17. The importance of confirmation risks appears to have grown in recent years. Looking at nominations to the Supreme Court, for example, the Bork and Ginsburg nominations by Ronald Reagan were watersheds. Following those two episodes, confirmability was critical for Reagan and Bush (the unforeseen Clarence Thomas controversy notwithstanding), and is perhaps even more so for Bill Clinton thus far.

18. Sheldon Goldman raises precisely this point in "Bush's Judicial Legacy: The Final Imprint," *Judicature* 76 (1993), 287.

19. Polsby, "The Institutionalization of the U.S. House of Representatives," 145.

20. J. Harvie Wilkinson III, "The Drawbacks of Growth in the Federal Judiciary," *Emory Law Journal* 43 (1994), 1147.

21. U.S. Senate Judiciary Committee, *Report on S. 2648: The Judicial Improvements Act of 1990* (Washington, D.C.: Government Printing Office, 1990), 34.

22. U.S. Senate Judiciary Committee, *Report on S. 2648,* 34.

23. U.S. Congress, General Accounting Office, *Federal Judiciary: How the Judicial Conference Assesses the Need for More Judges,* Report GAO/GDD-93-31 (Washington, D.C.: Government Printing Office, January 1993), 1–2, 12, 17.

24. This problem is exacerbated when vacancies go unfilled for extended periods of time. In 1993 the Alliance for Justice noted that: "Almost one-half of the vacancies now on the bench are more than two years old." See *Alliance for Justice Judicial Selection Project Annual Report, 1993,* (Washington, D.C.: Alliance for Justice, 1993), 9. The large number of judges who take senior status and thus still hear cases

ameliorates the problem, but the number of "judge years" will still decline if there is a large number of vacancies. See "Senior Judges Help District Courts Keep Pace," *The Third Branch* 26 (1994), 1.

25. See the classic treatments of James G. March and Herbert A. Simon, *Organizations* (New York: John Wiley & Sons, 1958); Victor A. Thompson, *Modern Organization* (New York: Alfred A. Knopf, 1961); and James D. Thompson, *Organizations in Action* (New York: McGraw-Hill, 1967). Nelson Polsby described how critical the socialization process was for the smooth functioning of the House; see "The Institutionalization of the U.S. House of Representatives," 164–68. For an application of socialization to a judicial setting, see Nancy Lenore Alpert, *The Judicial Career: Patterns of Socialization on the Bench*. Ph.D. diss., Northwestern University, Evanston, Illinois, 1981.

26. Wilkinson enumerates several such problems in "The Drawbacks of Growth in the Federal Judiciary." He believes that unbridled growth will lead to a breakdown of collegiality and the deliberative process that are at the heart of the responsibility to render legal precedent. The number of possible panel combinations would increase exponentially, which in turn would produce "a loss in the coherence of circuit law" (1174). Then, "[a]s the law of the circuit becomes murkier, litigation is increased" (1175), and so we have come full cycle. Bench expansion is not always the answer because, after all, "dispensing justice is very different from producing widgets" (1174).

27. Kenneth McNeil and James D. Thompson, "The Regeneration of Social Organizations," *American Sociological Review* 36 (1971), 628.

28. McNeil and Thompson, "The Regeneration of Social Organizations," 634.

29. Justice Felix Frankfurter, concurring in *Lumbermen's Casualty Co. v. Elbert*, 348 U.S. 48 (1954), at 59.

30. May 17, 1993, A11.

31. His essay was entitled, "Yes. More Would Dilute the Quality." A Democrat, Newman was appointed by President Carter in 1979.

32. For a dissenting view on this point see J. Clifford Wallace, "The Case for Large Federal Courts of Appeals," *Judicature* 77 (1994), 288.

33. This view is challenged, at least with reference to the Ninth Circuit, in Arthur Hellman, *Restructuring Justice* (Ithaca, N.Y.: Cornell University Press, 1990).

34. "Yes. More Would Dilute the Quality," A11.

35. "No. More Cases Should Be Heard." Reinhardt, also a Democrat, was appointed by President Carter in 1980.

36. "No. More Cases Should Be Heard," A11.

37. *Report of the Proceedings of the Judicial Conference of the United States*, March 16, 1993, 16.

38. *Report of the Proceedings of the Judicial Conference of the United States*, September 20, 1993, 51. According to David Sellers, a representative of the Administrative Office of the U.S. Courts who attended the meeting, the two-hour discussion could be characterized in those terms. "Keeping a Trim Federal Judiciary," *ABA Journal* 79 (1993), 26.

39. "Judicial Conference Endorses Carefully Controlled Court Growth," *The Third Branch* 25 (1993), 1.

40. *Report of the Proceedings of the Judicial Conference of the United States,* September 22, 1993, 69–71; March 16, 1993, 6; September 20, 1993, 51. Of the 29 temporary judgeships, 19 would be for the courts of appeals, with 6 permanent positions on the district courts, 5 new. The 6 permanent judgeships, if legislated, would be the fewest added in an omnibus bill since the Act of 1940. The recommendations of September 1994 increased the number of temporary appellate court judgeships to 20 and called for 18 permanent positions (3 conversions), and 5 temporary district court judgeships. *Report of the Proceedings of the Judicial Conference of the United States,* September 20, 1994, 53–54.

41. In 1988, Congress created within the Judicial Conference a 15-member Federal Courts Study Committee composed of judges, legislators, and private attorneys. Its 1990 report took a rather dim view of unlimited bench growth and instead focused on ways to ease the current pressures on the judiciary. One approach would be to limit the number of demands entering the federal judicial system by, for example, having Congress direct additional funds to state courts, who would then assume a larger responsibility in the areas of drugs and crime. Federal jurisdiction based on diversity of citizenship would also be limited, as would the removal from state to federal court of minor cases arising under the Employee Retirement Income Security Act, and the opportunities for case consolidation (both multiparty and multidistrict) would be increased. The committee also suggested that administrative proceedings could replace judicial ones in some areas (e.g., Social Security disability claims), at least at the hearing stage. And in areas such as tax and bankruptcy, trials could be heard by new complements of Article I judges. Congress paid considerable attention to administrative issues in its consideration of the Judicial Improvements Act of 1990, and adopted a number of proposals.

42. "The Drawbacks of Growth in the Federal Judiciary," 1163–64.

43. Carl Baar, *Judgeship Creation in the Courts: Options for Reform* (Washington, D.C.: Federal Judicial Center, 1981).

44. Baar, *Judgeship Creation in the Federal Courts,* 4.

45. Barrow and Zuk, "An Institutional Analysis of Turnover," 457–76.

46. See Goldman, "Bush's Judicial Legacy," 287, 293.

47. David R. Mayhew, *Congress: The Electoral Connection* (New Haven, Conn.: Yale University Press, 1974).

48. That is, the inclination of the president and Congress to expand federal jurisdiction and the consequent need to enlarge the bench (abetted by the Judicial Conference), and the increasing proclivity of judges to take advantage of attractive retirement options and so create vacancies.

49. See, for example, Paul D. Carrington, "Crowded Dockets and the Courts of Appeals: The Threat to the Function of Review and the National Law," *Harvard Law Review* 82 (1969): 542–617.

Index